Plan a Future that Sets You Free

How to Achieve Your Goals and Live the Life
You've Always Wanted

Lara Spadetto

Contents

To all those who open the drawer of forgotten dreams, and begin the journey.

"Do not follow where the path may lead. Go instead where there is no path and leave a trail."

—Ralph Waldo Emerson

Introduction

I can't pinpoint a moment when I realized I forgot what my dreams were. I don't think there was a precise moment; instead, it was a gradual process. Over time, as life continued its unstoppable course, as I was faced with unexpected responsibilities, and as I tried to cover others' expectations of who or what I should be, I found myself siphoning off the potency of my dreams. I told myself that sooner or later my time would come, until one day, I noticed that, at some point, I had put my goals and desires aside for so long that I had forgotten what they were.

According to a survey of the Global Dreams Index, a shocking reality emerges: Over half of the female population in the world has given up their dreams, to the point of leaving them dissatisfied with their lives (Gourani, 2019).

Reading that was shocking, but it made me realize that there were other women like me out there, far more than I had ever thought. Faced with this realization, I had to ask myself: Why do so many of us give up on our dreams?

I don't think there is an easy answer. For some, it may be a lack of resources or support, while others may have struggled with a life of hardship and trauma. It could be that other things took precedence, such as family, or the illness of a loved one.

Or it may simply be that we think we are not worth it; that we will never be able to reach the goals we set for ourselves, and so we give up sooner, to avoid a disappointment that we do not want to face. We give up to avoid a possible failure.

Have you been advised to take the easy way out? That what you dreamed of was too difficult? Have you been told to be more realistic? Maybe it was someone else who told you in the beginning, and then as the years went by, it became your own voice in your head, telling you to cut back on those dreams.

Don't get me wrong; the key point is just how we interpret the concept. We need to be practical, but only when planning how we can achieve our goals. And it's true, we have to be realistic, as nothing is given as a gift, and nothing comes as a miracle. You need to work hard, but working for something you are passionate about and love is much more fulfilling than working less, for something you don't like, and can barely stand.

But, above all, by giving up we not only deprive ourselves of the possible final prize, we also let go of the opportunity to enjoy the journey to reach it. And that journey is probably really the secret ingredient that can enrich our life.

I, like you, at some point, had to face my own life, my past choices, and the responsibility of the present ones. I had to confront the reality that having placed my dreams in a secret drawer entailed the danger of forgetting the existence of this hiding place with the risk, like many other women, of losing them forever.

I'd spent so much time shoving my hopes and desires to the back of my mind, that part of me had almost forgotten about them in the first place. What did I want my life to be like when I was six? Twelve? Twenty-five?

Bringing these desires back to the surface was like meeting myself again. It was hard in some moments, but extremely important to reconnect with those parts of me that I had neglected.

It is important to remember that there is no expiry date on your dreams. There is not an age, milestone, or stage in your life that is a point of no return. No matter how much you have been through, no matter how much you have pushed aside or given up, you can still live the life you want.

If for a long time you have put the needs of others as a priority, it is difficult to change, but doing so does not mean neglecting those close to you. On the contrary, making this change is an act of love, for both you, as well as them. As I began working toward my long-forgotten goals, I felt a sense of hope and wholeness arise within me again.

When you commit to chasing your dreams, you'll begin to see all the good that comes from creating the future you've always envisioned. The most significant benefit is that following your dreams makes life worth living.

So often, you can fall into the trap of habit. Each day merges with the next, and you live this routine feeling that something is missing, but without realizing what it is.

We don't take the time to think, we don't have the time to think, and each day follows the one before.

I think it happens when we lose sight of our purpose. We run every day to fulfill all our responsibilities, but we neglect the responsibility we have toward ourselves.

When you start pursuing your goals; when you have a purpose, it's like you've been given a paddle. Suddenly you are in control of the direction of your life, and you can choose where to go.

By chasing your dreams, you grant meaning to your life. Be they big dreams or small ones, having a goal keeps you moving forward. Dreams are, in many ways, what can keep you going in life, giving you a shining beacon to work toward in both the good and bad times.

Pursuing your goals can also help you prove yourself. There's something so satisfying about imagining proving all the people who told you to give up wrong. Just remember, though, that their opinions shouldn't define your success. Achieving your goals is also a way to prove to yourself that you are strong, capable, and deserving of living a life of happiness. It's a way to show that negative voice in your head that it's wrong.

Following your dreams can be an incredible source of pride. We are often told not to fly too high and to keep our feet on the ground, so it is assumed that some objectives are too difficult to achieve, and therefore must be resized at the origin. Self-confidence is often confused with arrogance, but you should be proud of yourself, and feel confident in your abilities. When you achieve your goals, you're proving to yourself what you already knew: That you are someone who can do amazing things.

Remember, too, that you only have one life to live. This is your life, and being the only one, at least with these characteristics, you should choose carefully what you want to do, because what you do, first, defines your own perception of yourself. Don't worry about what other people think. Look inside yourself, and see if your life brings you joy. If not, I think it's time for you to start making a cha nge.

I've been where you are. I know what it's like to feel unfulfilled in life; to have decided that your dreams were somehow less valuable or important than someone else's. I know how it feels to wonder if it's too late to start living your dreams.

Living a life filled with my dreams, goals, and desires wasn't an overnight journey. It took time, mistakes, and a lot of hard work. However, I can confidently say that this journey was worth every moment.

In this book, I'll take you through everything I've learned during my journey. I'll show you how to recognize the good in your life that already exists, how to understand the parts of your life that need work, as well as how to plan for a future that brings you excitement and joy so you, too, can achieve your goals and long-held desires, leading you toward a life that sets you free.

Chapter 1

Past

Recognize Your Accomplishments

*"Every great accomplishment rests on the
foundation of what came before it; when you
trace it back, you'll see one small step that started
it all."*

—Stephen Guise

L ife, at the beginning of our journey, seems infinite.
Rationally, we know that one day it will end, but we see
this end as a very distant thing. We think we have all the
time in the world to make our dreams come true and have
the life we want. We relegate our dreams to the back of our
minds, and we live everyday life continuing to think that it
will be forever.

The habit and security of what is known takes over. The fear
of losing this security holds us back, or perhaps it is the fear
of possible disappointment or failure. These things keep

us away from what we aspired to, and we see it becoming distant without knowing what to do.

One day something happens that makes us recap; something that upsets our plans. It is a turning point, often hurtful, but it hits us with a force that causes a change of perspective on the vision of our life.

It is ironic to think that we constantly try to avoid suffering, but it is precisely the hardest and most painful moments that can make us open our eyes. It's like getting a slap in the face that wakes you up from numbness.

It is clear that at that point, there may be two things to do. We can feel sorry for ourselves and despair about everything we have not been able to do, or we can remind ourselves of everything we already have, as well as our abilities, and define more precisely what we want to achieve in the future from this point.

Evaluating what you have accomplished is a good starting point for defining what you still want to attain. After all, there's a good chance you've already made some dreams that you may not have even realized had come true.

———————◆○◆———————

Understanding What You've Already Achieved

It's so easy to become caught up in ruminations surrounding what you don't have, or what you have not done in life. There's no denying the role our society plays in this mindset. We're constantly bombarded by things like advertising and social media telling us that other people have it better than us, and that something is missing from our lives.

Falling into this trap will only demoralize you. Obsessing over the accomplishments of others and comparing them to yourself blinds you to the good that already exists in your life. This is why it's essential to focus on your life, not the lives of others, or even the idealized version of life that you might have once invented in your head.

Taking the time to look at the reality of your situation can lead to incredible insights. When you allow yourself to understand and bask in the reality of the present situation, you can better understand who you are as a person, and where you are in your life.

Reflect, as well, on what is important to you as you are now. After all, we're constantly changing. I'm not the same person I was five, ten, fifteen years ago, and I'm sure you aren't either. As we change as people, so too do our dreams. What mattered to us when we were younger might not matter the same way now, as our priorities in life shift. Taking the time to examine what we value now can help us understand which dreams still matter to us, and whether there are new goals we would like to strive for.

This is, in my opinion, such an important thing to remember. While I wholeheartedly believe in the power that pursuing your dreams gives you, I also believe in the power of letting go of goals that no longer fit you and your needs. It's all too easy to become blinded by the past and hold firm to a dream we once had. This can lead you down a path not to joy, but instead to pain. Taking the time to reflect on what dreams align with your current values is a simple way to avoid that fate.

When you're reflecting on your life as it is now, consider all aspects of your life. Unexpected accomplishments are hiding around every corner, and many of them are things we tell ourselves anyone would do, thereby minimizing their impact in our minds. Here are a few areas of your life you should look to when reflecting on what you have already achieved in life:

Career

Your career is an easy place to find achievements, both expected and unexpected. Consider the job you have. Even if it isn't your dream job, it's still a place that you might have worked hard to reach.

That hard work is something to take pride in! Maybe you played an essential role in getting a project done, or you helped out another coworker when they needed assistance with something. Perhaps you have a great relationship with your coworkers. These are only a few examples of successes you can have in your career that aren't the typical "dream job" accomplishment.

Home and Family

Your home life is another place filled with achievements, and it's particularly undervalued. Having a healthy home life can be challenging. It's all too easy to overlook your home as you become caught up in all the other aspects of life. However, maintaining a happy and healthy home is undoubtedly an accomplishment.

Your familial relationships, as well, are a point of pride. Take being a mom, for example. It's a lot of work, and since being a good mom is the standard, it's all too easy to brush that off. But being a good mom is a huge achievement, and is something that you should celebrate. Even if you don't have kids, having a good relationship with your family is an accomplishment. Take pride in being a good child or good sibling, and supporting your loved ones.

Friendships

Being a good friend is also an achievement that we downplay. Think about your treasured friends, and how much you appreciate their presence in your lives. Now, think about what you would say if they downplayed their abilities as a friend. You'd want to tell them to be proud of themselves, right? Well, that's the same mentality you should have for yourself. Think about the times you've been there for others, even when it was something small, like buying them a coffee when they had a bad day. Those acts of genuine love, caring, and kindness all add up over time, and those acts should be remembered.

How You Respond to Setbacks

Your actions, as well, are ways you can discover achievements you might not have known about. Think about a time you were faced with hardship in life, and how you were able to move past those troubling times. The simple act of making it through a difficult period of life is, in my opinion, an achievement in and of itself. What's even more impressive is when we manage to rise above those times, and not let them hold us back as we move forward in our lives.

The ability to get back up when you fall is an accomplishment. It's hard to pick yourself back up and be willing to face challenges head-on. It takes courage to keep trying and face adversity when success is not guaranteed. When you respond to failure with determination, that's an accomplishment, often overshadowed by the original unsuccessful attempt.

13

Your Character

Standing up for your beliefs and maintaining your integrity is another huge accomplishment. Living according to your values can sometimes be tricky, as life so often challenges those values. When you refuse to bend to the whims of the world, instead choosing to stand firm against the storm, you show your strength of character and, in many ways, act as a role model for others.

Being genuine and authentic in your interactions with others, and being deliberate and true to yourself in your choices and actions speaks to who you are, and validates your successes in many ways. When you achieve something while being true to yourself, it makes the accomplishment feel more genuine, as it shows that you can achieve great things while maintaining your integrity and values.

These are only a few examples of the areas of your life you should look to when reflecting on what you have already accomplished in life. Some of them may feel small, especially when you compare them to the grandiose dreams that so often define childhood, but they are anything but small. Simple acts of kindness can make all the difference in someone else's life, so you should take pride in everything you have already done. Celebrate yourself for the beautiful person that you already are!

When you understand what you have already done, you can begin to plan for your future goals. By looking at what you have achieved, you can recognize the happiness in your life. This means that your future plans and goals aren't going to make or break the level of fulfillment you already have in life. Rather than being the key to finding joy in life, your future plans will enhance the wonderful life you already have.

How Society Tells Us No

When thinking about dreams you might have set aside, it's important to remember not to place all the blame on your own shoulders. While we are all responsible for our life choices, outside forces can play a huge role in what we decide.

As a woman, there's a good chance you have experienced varying degrees of sexism in the face of your goals. It's even likely that you've faced sexism without even realizing it. Gender biases are so ingrained in our society that they're normalized, and often accepted as common knowledge. These inherent biases unknowingly shape the way we view ourselves and others, and can, whether we want them to or not, influence the choices we make.

If you think of a pilot, painter, chef, nurse, doctor, secretary, or caregiver, who do you see in your mind? There's a good chance you pictured a woman in the more nurturing roles, with men in the leadership roles. It's an unfortunate reality of life that we inevitably and involuntarily give gender to that job without thinking about it. This gendering of careers is, for many of us, the result of years of brainwashing.

Think about it, and ask yourself: How many clichés surround women's abilities? I find it rather strange that in many areas, it is still difficult to find prominent female names, and the times when we do, they're seen as something of an outlier.

Take the world of art, and try to think of how many artists' names come to your mind, and how many of these are female. The same goes for the world of science, and mathematics. Ask yourself: How many internationally renowned chefs are women? How many film directors? While there are prominent women making strides in these sectors, they're still vastly underrepresented.

In STEM fields —STEM meaning science, technology, engineering, and mathematics, for those of you who may not know— in particular, there is a large gap in the gender divide of workers. In fact, according to research conducted by the American Association of University Women, commonly referred to as AAUW, only 28% of workers in STEM are women. When you break down these percentages by each field, some of the divides are even more stark, such as in engineering fields, where women only make up 16.5% of the workforce.

It's about more than the workforce, though. It starts earlier than that, from when we're just young girls. When we look at the statistics surrounding post-secondary students majoring in STEM fields, there's still a large discrepancy in the numbers. Only 19% of computer science students are women, and of that 19%, only 38% work in the computer field (AAUW, 2020).

This is the case across the board for women. Even in fields where there is a more even split, such as healthcare fields, the executive positions aren't held by women. As such, even when women are represented in terms of numbers, they still aren't represented in terms of power.

On top of all this, many times we can have internalized misogyny not only toward ourselves, but also toward other women, especially in the workforce. Often, women are socialized to see each other not as allies, but as competition. Even if you've made an effort to go against this social conditioning, those old thoughts can creep back in, and you may find yourself thinking less about the women around you without meaning to.

To eradicate this concept, we must first start.

When we don't know something is wrong, there's no way we can do anything to fix the situation. Once you discover the problem, though, you can begin to make changes. So, if you encountered any of these cultural structures that contributed to you not chasing your dreams, don't beat yourself up. Instead, reach within yourself and find the determination and strength that has always been there. Then, take that strength and prove society wrong by living the life of your dreams; a life without any gender biases or limitations.

Why Women Often Give Up on Their Dreams

Even beyond societal biases and expectations, all kinds of other internal and external factors might have prompted you to give up on some of your dreams. Your perspective on life, and the perspective of those around you, might have played a prominent role.

You become accustomed to living a certain way, and you grow comfortable with your position in life. The idea of potentially giving up on certain things, or even sacrificing elements of your comfortable life to chase your dreams, is frightening. It can be a deterrent for many people, men and women alike.

Why, then, is it overwhelmingly women who are more likely to give up some of their life goals? It is not easy to answer this question, and perhaps there is no single answer, but I think there are a few key reasons why women often are the ones who sacrifice some of their goals.

A Historical Basis

History may play a significant role in a woman's decision not to pursue specific life goals. Looking back at times past, women often had to be dependent on men for security in life. They couldn't support themselves without a man for the most part, and the women who could do so were few and far between.

While this has shifted as time has moved forward, these attitudes still linger in many of us. Our parents and grandparents were potentially raised on those ideals, and may have unknowingly instilled that mindset into us. This is why it is essential to look beyond just the choices you made and try to find the root cause that prompted you to make those choices.

Lack of Support

Just as a garden needs good soil, water, and sunlight to grow, people need a support system to flourish. Being independent doesn't mean being alone, nor does it mean doing everything yourself without anyone's help. The reality of the world is that none of us are alone. Humans are meant to share their lives with others in order to become their best selves.

It's much harder to achieve your goals when you don't have a strong support system. Having people around you supporting your dreams will make you more likely to pursue those dreams in the first place, and since women are often told to be realistic with their ambitions, that support often isn't there.

But it's more than that. Having people who encourage you to pursue your passions in the first place is incredibly helpful, but it's just as essential to have role models or mentors who can guide you on your journey. If there aren't people in your life who can, to some extent, help show you the way forward, this journey becomes significantly more challenging.

Not having support is incredibly demoralizing. It creeps into your mind and, over time, can convince you that following your passions isn't worth the effort. Eventually, you let that doubt creep in, and decide to stop chasing these goals. This is why having a solid support system is so essential. After all, if you want to follow your dreams, grow, and thrive in life, you need support, same as everyone else.

Low Self-Esteem

Another key element of choosing to chase your dreams is having the confidence to do so. When you don't believe in yourself, you set yourself up for failure. It's like going into a job interview with the preconceived idea that it will not go well. There's no way that negative mindset won't translate to your performance, and it becomes a self-fulfilling prophecy. You tell yourself you won't succeed, and so you don't.

A lack of belief in yourself and your capabilities can infect your mind, sometimes even going so far as to convince you that it isn't even worth trying to pursue your goals in the first place.

When you find yourself thinking this way, it's essential to stop those thoughts in their tracks. Remember that low self-esteem doesn't define you. Even if you don't believe it, you are more than capable of achieving your goals in life. The only thing that listening to the unconfident voice in your head will do is hold you back. By deciding to believe in yourself, you'll find that accomplishing your dreams is well within your reach.

Unfulfilling Jobs

If your passions lie outside of the traditional nine to five corporate career, there's a good chance you're supporting yourself with a job you don't necessarily care too much about. With such an emphasis on the importance of careers, more and more people define themselves by their job title. If you work a job that you don't love, that can be incredibly draining mentally, emotionally, and even physically!

It's vital to remember that it is normal for people to work jobs that aren't that important to them to make sure they're financially stable. The majority of people are likely doing this. So long as you don't allow a job you don't love to take over your life, there's nothing wrong with your passions lying elsewhere.

However, the problem is that jobs like these can begin to take over our lives. You can feel exhausted after an unfulfilling day at work. When you get home, you might not even want to engage in a creative endeavor, for example. Instead, you might want to curl up on your couch and turn your brain off for a few hours.

While taking a break is healthy, the problem arises when these days change from being once in a while to daily occurrences. If your job is draining your energy, leaving you with nothing left for the other areas of your life, you need to take a step back and re-evaluate a few things.

Gratitude journaling is a great way to deal with this strain on your life. If you aren't finding fulfillment from your job, then you can instead take the time to practice shifting your focus to finding fulfillment in other areas of your life. Maybe your job isn't great, but your coworkers are. Maybe there's a coffee shop you love near your workplace. Perhaps you work from home and get to go for walks in your neighborhood during your lunch hour.

Whatever the case may be, finding things in your day that make your life brighter can help stave off the adverse effects of working a job you don't like. This, in turn, will help you to keep your energy up, so you can focus on what truly matters to you.

A Lack of Organization

A lack of organization can play a huge role in why you might have given up on particular ambitions. Sometimes, what you want out of life takes a lot of planning. If you aren't the type of person to make plans, it's all too easy to feel overwhelmed by your goals. You lose sight of your dream, too bogged down by the minutiae you don't know how to deal with.

I also urge you to keep in mind that chasing your dreams and knowing what you want in life aren't restricted to age. How old you are shouldn't affect your ability to plan for your future and pursue your goals. Young or old, you should do your best to figure out what you want in life.

Once you know what you want, you can make a plan for your future. After all, when you understand how you can make room for your dreams within your life, the way forward becomes clear. Looking at your life and seeing where you can grow and make changes is helpful, no matter your goals.

21

Your Dreams Changed

Another big reason you might have given up on your dreams is that they changed. I don't think a single person out there hasn't changed their mind about what they want out of life. I know I certainly have!

If what you once thought you wanted isn't what you still want, that's perfectly fine! If you found yourself at a point where your priorities shifted, and you gave up on dreams you once had in order to pursue new ones, that's not a failure—that's an overwhelming success!

For a lot of people, starting a family is one of those dreams. Maybe you dreamed about being a famous artist when you were a child. Then, as you grew older, those dreams shifted. Instead of what you once dreamed of, you realized you wanted to have children and be a good parent. That's an admirable dream, and it's so meaningful, fulfilling, and rewarding.

Remember, though, that you can always go back to your dreams. There is absolutely nothing stopping you from being both a mom and an artist if that's what would add joy to your life. After all, pursuing one dream doesn't mean sacrificing another.

These are only a few reasons why someone might decide to give up on pursuing specific goals. There are all kinds of internal and external factors in your life. I encourage you to reflect on these factors, and see which might stand in the way of achieving your dreams, both past and present.

As we go through this book, I encourage you to start a notebook. Laying out your thoughts through the written word is a great way to see your progress and organize your ideas, in order to better understand yourself.

Try writing down all of your accomplishments, for example. Include every award you've ever won, even things from your childhood! I suggest you include personal achievements as well. Buying your first home, getting a promotion, and moving to a new city are examples of successes you might have already experienced.

Seeing this list is a great way to show yourself all you have done at every stage in your life. It's a reminder that, throughout your life, you have always had the power within you to make all your dreams come true.

Through this, you'll see that you are ready to make those first steps in your journey toward achieving your goals. There isn't anything inside you that's lacking. All you need is to know how to plan for your future, and start implementing those plans in your life.

Chapter 2

Present

Take Stock of What You Have

"Money is only a tool. It will take you wherever you wish, but it will not replace you as the driver."

—Ayn Rand

When you start a new stage in your life, it's like embarking on a journey. You have to plan it, and even if you like adventure, you have to know where you start from, what you should bring with you, and what you have available to bring along in the first place. In your baggage there is not only clothes, documents, and money, there is also something invisible—but critical—and that is your experience.

We never start from a point "zero." I realized this when I took stock of my life. And though the feeling I had was to start all over again, it wasn't like that, because I realized: Everything I had experienced before this point was there to help me, and make me feel stronger. Everything I actually had was there, too, and taking stock of my life—making a literal list—helped me to access a clearer vision of where I was in the path of my life. Above all, though, it helped me to start clarifying what the next step I wanted to take was.

I was afraid, obviously. I felt anxiety due to uncertainty, and I felt insecurity in my abilities; afraid of losing even what I still had. But at that point, I realized that by doing nothing, I would have lost much more.

I know, now, that I wasn't alone in this experience. A big reason so many people feel hesitant about chasing their dreams in the first place is due to finances. If you were ever told to be realistic, was it also followed up by people asking if you thought your passions were something that could make you a living? Financial considerations are undeniably important, but the thing most people forget to say is that, with a bit of planning, you can make your dreams and your money work for you.

Don't let fear of not having enough money hold you back from what you want in life. Money isn't the end goal in life. Instead, it's simply a way for you to further your goals.

Things like financial literacy, understanding your personal finances, and learning how to manage your money seem daunting. I'll go through everything I've learned about the importance of knowing your personal finances, so you can see that these financial barriers aren't as overwhelming as you might have once thought they were.

Understanding Your Personal Finances

When you understand your finances, you free yourself from the anxiety surrounding money. Your personal finances are how you manage your money and everything that goes along with that, from investments to taxes to mortgages, and more.

In many ways, your personal finances and financial planning go hand in hand, as personal finances are a way of making and meeting financial goals. There are so many ways in which understanding your personal finances is essential to planning for your future. When you make your personal finances work for you, you pull down financial barriers, and achieve your version of financial freedom.

Here are a few of the benefits that come from understanding your personal finances:

Meeting Your Monetary Needs

There's more to your monetary needs than a lot of people think. There are bills, of course, but there are also rent or mortgage payments, groceries, home supplies, and money for entertainment and fun. In an ideal world, you wouldn't have to spend so much of your paycheck once you receive it, but that isn't the reality for many of us.

Understanding your personal finances offers insight into how much you make versus how much you spend. You can then create a financial plan that keeps track of your income, expenses, objectives, and future goals.

Understanding your personal finances will also help you see that you can manage your monetary needs. It keeps your money from becoming something overwhelming and stress-inducing. It takes back control of your money, and returns it to your hands in many ways.

When you look at your financial state, you can see the areas where you can make room for pursuing your dreams. Sometimes you might need to reorganize your expenses, but that isn't bad. Reprioritizing your finances can help you see areas where you might have been overspending out of habit.

Managing Your Income

When you have a plan for your personal finances, you can more easily manage your income. Understanding which parts of your income you should save, spend, budget, and invest will help you make room in your life for your future plans.

The great thing about our current technological society is that it provides you with all kinds of opportunities to find multiple streams of income, all from the comfort of your home. After all, in these times, it's important to try and find more than one stream of income. I would honestly recommend looking into at least five different threads. These can include jobs, investments, selling things online, and more.

The opportunities presented by the internet makes that so much easier. Consider looking into online opportunities for yourself to see if there are any you can take advantage of, in order to supplement your personal finances.

Understanding Budgets

Having a reasonable budget can make all the difference in managing your money. Not only does it help you keep track of what you should spend, but it also helps you keep track of when you should spend. Knowing when all your bills are due, and incorporating that into your financial plans, makes it easier to make room in your budget for the fun stuff!

If you have a big goal, like buying a new car or going on a trip, having a budget can help you stay on track and meet the monetary needs of that goal. Knowing how to keep track of and stick to a budget is also a way to prepare yourself for achieving your goals, as it gives you experience with planning, preparation, and following through on your plans.

Helps Manage Debt

Debt is one of the biggest causes of stress, and is one of the tallest financial barriers that stand in the way of someone's dreams.

Once you're in debt, it can feel as though there's nothing you can do but fall deeper into it. You start to see any debt as overwhelming; just another weight dragging you down. But that isn't the case! Some debt is not a problem, and understanding your finances can help you learn to manage your debt.

In time, you can throw off the chains of debt and keep it from growing into an insurmountable hurdle. Don't put off taking care of debt because it's stressful! Instead, take the time to look at your debts, and find a way you can incorporate managing them into your budgets and financial plans so you can, one day, gain complete financial freedom.

Offers Familial Security

Understanding your finances does more than just help you learn to manage your money. It also has the potential to improve your way of life. By caring for your finances, you are caring for the security of your loved ones, as you are ensuring a sort of financial safety net you and your family can fall back on if ever there is such a need.

Ensuring the financial needs of your loved ones are met can lift a burden from your shoulders, one you might not have even known was there. While you can never plan for every hardship life might potentially put in your path, knowing that your family will be taken care of financially can help you prepare to navigate any unforeseen situations.

Taking the time to understand and master your personal finances is a huge step in securing and planning for your future. Your goals, dreams, and ambitions don't have to take a back seat to your immediate financial needs, so long as you learn how to manage your money. After all, achieving everything you want is much easier, more manageable, and well within your reach with sound financial management.

Take a Financial Inventory

Now that you know the benefits of learning about and understanding your personal finances, the next step is to look at your money and take a financial inventory. A financial inventory is exactly what it sounds like—it's when you go through all of your finances, compiling a complete list of your bills, expenses, debts, assets, and everything else that accompanies your personal finances.

That sounds so daunting. For many people, taking a financial inventory is one of the most stressful things you can do. Even saying the words can make hearts beat faster, and palms start to sweat. But it doesn't have to be that way.

From my experience, I've found that breaking down your financial inventory into smaller, more manageable pieces can help eliminate that anxiety, and help keep you on track throughout the process. By tackling one task at a time, instead of trying to do everything at once, your head will be clearer, and you can stay focused and make an accurate analysis of your personal finances.

The Three Questions

When taking a financial inventory, your first step is to ask yourself three simple, yet essential questions. The first question is: "How much money do I have?" Knowing how much money you have, in total, is the starting line across all your accounts. It's your baseline, your beginning point, and it's from here that you can begin to build upon your inventory.

The second question is: "How much money do I earn?" This question helps you see the influx of wealth you are receiving, and is a way for you to see the potential growth of your finances.

Finally, the third question is: "How much money do I owe?" This is perhaps the most important of the three questions, as it is often what you need to take care of sooner rather than later. Knowing how much money you owe is vital to weigh against your current finances and your future income. By looking at all three together, you can see where you are, financially speaking, and what direction you need to start taking as you build your financial plan.

Eliminate the Feeling of Being Overwhelmed

The next step is to find a method of doing your financial inventory that will work with your life and schedule in a way that isn't too overwhelming and energy draining. When you

31

have the time, a good one that I recommend is to work in 20 to 30 minute stretches.

Set a timer for the time period, and work throughout that whole block. Since it's at most half an hour, it will be easy to focus during that time. Stop what you're doing once the timer goes off, and take a break between 10 and 15 minutes.

If you have more time, work for another 20 to 30 minute stretch, making sure to keep taking those breaks in between. By giving yourself half-hour stretches in which to work, you minimize the anxiety that accompanies complex tasks that you know will take plenty of focus. Also, knowing that you only have a set amount of time in which to work can keep you motivated on the task before you, lessening the likelihood of your mind wandering, and becoming distracted.

What to Include in Your Lists

When doing a complete financial inventory, there are many factors to consider. During these half-hour periods, you're going to be writing many lists. These lists can be separated into a few different categories, the most important being what you own and what you owe.

Assets

Start by compiling a list of all your assets. This list should include all your financial accounts, like your checking and savings accounts. Any bank accounts you have open should go on this list.

Also, include your investments accounts, retirement accounts, any education accounts you might have, and a list of any real estate you own. Other assets you might have include cars, jewelry, or similar items.

In essence, this list will be all the finances you would include in what you own.

Liabilities

Next, make a list of all your financial liabilities. These include things like your credit cards and your debts, such as mortgages, personal loans, student loans, and auto loans.

This list will make up the bulk of what you owe. However, when calculating what you owe, be sure also to include monthly bills, like your internet, rent, and other amenities.

Insurance

If you have any insurance policies, be sure to include them in a list. This can cover life, car, homeowner's, health, and disability insurance policies.

Insurance policies can be paid monthly, every six months, or even yearly. Knowing when you have to pay each of your insurance premiums will help you stay on top of that expense.

This list should also be included in the category of what you owe.

Other Important Documents

Depending on your situation, you should include other important documents in your financial inventory like medical records, tax records, and military records. Your personal legal documents should also be included, even if they don't directly affect your current wealth and net worth. These documents include things like wills, power of attorney, landlord-tenant contracts, and any other legal documents that may, at some point, play a role in your fin ances.

LARA SPADETTO

Calculating Your Net Worth

Once you've compiled your lists, you'll need to calculate the totals of what you own and what you owe. When you've found these totals, subtract what you owe from what you own. That number represents your approximate net worth.

There's a chance you might find yourself in the negatives after this. If that's the case for you, don't panic. Remember, you are still likely receiving an inflow of cash from your job or other sources of income. Besides, this is if you have to pay everything all at once, which you don't have to do.

This isn't meant to freak you out; it's meant to show you where you're starting. Understanding your current net worth will help you plan for your future, and it is the first step to creating and managing a realistic, workable budget.

Completing a financial inventory is a way for you to take control of your finances and start to stay on top of them. This gives you more financial freedom, which, in turn, grants you the opportunity to pursue your goals.

If, however, you find yourself without extra money, don't despair! You can still pursue your goals, it might just take a few additional steps. Instead of forgoing your passions, see it as a chance for you to start working on a financial plan for your future.

34

Tips for Saving Money

A big part of getting on top of your finances is learning the best ways to save money. This is especially important when you're saving up for something big. In your case, that's probably saving up for your future plans and pursuits, whatever they may be.

Where to start saving? One idea may be to cut back on eating out and opting to have coffee at home, and while these are definitely ways to save money, they're not the only ones.

Here are some great ways you can start to save money, so you can put your plans for life into action:

Pay Yourself First

You've probably heard people say that you should put 20 percent of your paycheck into savings. While that isn't necessarily a bad practice, that much isn't feasible for everyone. The idea of paying yourself first—putting part of your income into a savings account—is one of the best ways to start saving money. However, the amount that you save depends on your financial situation.

Determine how much you can afford to save, and start with that, even if the amount seems small. After all, some savings are better than no savings, right? These small amounts will accrue in time, and you'll find your money increasing slowly but surely.

Open a Savings Account

An essential saving aid is making sure you have a savings account in the first place! There can be different types of savings accounts depending on the country you live in, so it's essential to take a look and see which of these accounts best suits you and your needs.

The purpose of the savings account is to create a source to draw from over time, when you need it, to achieve your goals. But it also serves the purpose of having a fund available in case of unforeseen events. This helps you have some mental peace of mind.

Save Little and Often

An increasingly popular method of saving your money is to practice something known as microsaving. This practice involves regularly putting away small amounts of money, typically once or twice a week.

This is an excellent savings method for people who don't have a lot of disposable income, as it only takes small amounts of money to put this method into practice. When you save little and often in this way, you are still creating savings, while getting into the habit of saving your money. When you find yourself in a better financial situation, saving your money will be like second nature to you, even if there is more money to save.

Use Automated Transfers

Setting up automated transfers between your checking and savings accounts can help you grow your wealth without even having to remember to do so. There are so many great tools to make transferring money from one account to another so much easier these days, so try to make the most of them.

This is especially helpful if you're the forgetful type. So often, we want to be good about setting a portion of our paychecks aside, but we completely forget when the time comes. By simplifying the process, you can stay on top of your money while also managing all the other things you have to juggle in life. This frees up time, energy, and brainpower for different activities, and can eliminate the stress that accompanies trying to remember if you've set aside your savings or not.

Prepare Before Shopping

Preparing before you shop is another great and easy way to save money. Looking for coupons, making lists, and seeing what you already have in your house can keep you from overspending on unnecessary purchases in the store.

This is particularly true for grocery shopping. Take a look at your pantry and fridge before heading out to the store, to remind yourself of what you already have at home. This way, if you see a familiar product in the store, you won't buy it out of habit.

If you're in charge of the meals and groceries in your home, making a meal plan for the week can help you manage your grocery shopping. Deciding on your dinners in advance means you only have to go shopping once a week, and you can grab everything you need all at once, rather than making a trip to the store every other day.

After all, the more often we're in the store, the more likely we're going to make impulse purchases. By eliminating how often you get groceries, you also eliminate that risk.

Map Out Major Purchases

If you have some major purchases on the horizon, it's good to plan to make those purchases during big sales. You will find better deals on electronics in November, for example, as opposed to purchasing them in, say, April.

You can also map out your significant purchases by looking at when you might have bigger payments due. If you pay your insurance premiums on a yearly basis, try to avoid major purchases at the same time that you're making those sorts of payments.

Look Into Lowering Payments

If you feel your bills have gone up, see if there's a way you can lower them! This can include making changes in your home—remembering to turn off the lights when you leave the room, for example—or it can mean changing your service providers for things like insurance or your internet.

Some of your expenses can even be refinanced, such as loan payments and mortgages. Take a look, and see if that's a good option for you!

Cancel Unnecessary Subscriptions

It's happened to me, and it's probably happened to you as well—you sign up for a free trial, and then, when the trial ends, you completely forget to cancel the subscription. With more and more subscription services, this is a trap that's all too easy to fall into.

I'd suggest setting a reminder somewhere, maybe on your calendar or phone, for the day your free trial ends. That way, if you find you aren't interested in continuing the subscription, you won't forget to cancel the trial.

Track Your Spending

Tracking your spending is one of the best ways to stay on top of your savings. The ideal amount of spending is to make sure that you always spend less than you earn. While that isn't always possible, it's certainly a good goal to strive for.

When you track your spending, you'll see the areas where you might be overspending. You can consider your purchases, and where you're spending the most money. Understanding where your money is going can help you determine which expenses should be prioritized. This understanding can then help you make a realistic budget that works for you.

Creating a Budget

Speaking of budgets, it can be challenging to know where to start when actually making one! An easy budget template that I halfway referenced earlier is the 50/30/20 budgeting framework. This takes into account the three primary budgeting needs—that is, your needs, your wants, and your savings.

Your needs include things you need to pay. This includes groceries, mortgages, rent, and other necessary costs. According to this budget template, you should set aside 50 percent of your paycheck for your needs.

Then, there are your wants. This is sometimes also called discretionary spending, and it covers purchases that you don't need, but do want. This includes eating out, seeing movies, or making purchases for your hobbies. For some of you, this part of your income is also what you might spend on funding your dreams. For your wants, try to set aside 30 percent of your paycheck.

Finally, there are the savings. With this framework, you should set the last 20 percent of your paycheck aside for your savings. I mentioned this earlier, however, and said that you should determine how much you put in your savings based on your individual needs. I believe that's true for all parts of this framework. You don't have to stick to the 50/30/20 rule. Instead, try to adapt the percentages for what best suits your lifestyle.

When creating your budget, it's essential to determine how much you will make and receive each month. Keeping track of your cash flow, both in and out, will help you see how best to structure your budget. I've included an easy template at the end of this chapter, as an example of how to keep track of your money each month. You can copy this or download it by following the link at the end of the book.

Add up all your income and all your expenses, and see the totals you have for each month. Then, take a look at the difference column. See where you might have spent more or less than you budgeted, and, if you feel it's necessary, make adjustments in your budget for the next month.

This table is, as I said, only a template. You can adapt it and its contents to fit your personal financial needs. However, seeing your money laid out like this can help you see the best ways for you to move forward financially.

As you can see, financial worries don't have to be a reason for you to set aside your ambitions. Taking the time to understand and get on top of your finances will help you find a way to make your money work for, and support you, as you pursue your dreams—and not the other way around.

Money Track

Month of _____

	Budget	Actual	Difference
Income			
Paycheck			
Investments			
Saving			
Other			
Total Income			
House Exp.			
Mortgage/Rent			
Utilities			
Insurance			
Living Exp.			
Groceries			
Gas/Transport			
Personal			
Entertainment			
Vacation			
Debt			
Loans			
Insurance			
Credit Card			
Total Exp.			

Total Income _____ − Total Expences _____

= Total _____

Money Tracker

.

Chapter 3

Future

Understand What You Want

"The world needs dreamers and the world needs doers. But above all, the world needs dreamers who do."

—*Sarah Ban Breathnach*

U nderstanding what we want is not as easy as it sounds. Have you ever thought about what you would wish for if you found the genie's lamp from Aladdin? Try it now. Once you have decided what your main desires are, can you adequately tell yourself what it is you're willing to do in order to achieve them? Because letting your imagination go, and wandering around in parallel worlds is one thing—but defining what makes you feel happy, satisfied with yourself, and above all, what you are willing to devote time, work, energy, and passion to—is another.

It's easy to say you're going to follow your dreams, but it's harder sometimes to know what your dreams are. You might know what you wanted when you were younger, but do those wants still ring true in your heart? Do they still drive the force of your soul? Sometimes the things we once dreamed of accomplishing no longer bring us passion.

On the same track, sometimes we forget the dreams we once cherished. For some people, and maybe for you as well, so much time has passed that you can't remember all of your previous ambitions.

Re-discovering old dreams and discovering new goals are necessary for planning your future. After all, without an understanding of what you want, you won't know how to choose the path forward, nor will you know how to lay the foundations of this path in the first place.

Even after deciding to pursue your passions, and even after looking at your finances and making room for your goals, if you don't know the shape your ambitions take, you can't make progress in achieving anything. This is why you must turn your gaze inward, and look inside yourself. Taking the time to reflect on your desires will help you understand what you want for your future.

I must confess that it took me a while to figure out what I wanted. With a little patience and openness to what the world was offering me, I eventually became convinced that when we open ourselves up to the opportunities that are out there, they somehow come knocking on our door. It is up to us to open up that door, and let them in.

⬤

The Five Step Method to Understanding Your Inner Truths

When you're ready to start the self-reflection necessary to understand your ambitions, try this five-step method to look inside yourself and discover your actual wants, needs, and desires.

These five steps are a great way to connect with yourself and gain a more profound knowledge of your core values. In many ways, these five steps are an outline you can use for building your plans for the future in general, as they cover all the bases you need to start your journey.

Throughout this chapter, and the rest of the book, I'll guide you through these five steps, going in-depth so that by the end, you'll be more than ready to start heading toward the future of your dreams.

Step One: Start With the Little Things

The first step includes looking at your life as it is, much as I went over previously. Take a look at what you have already accomplished, and see which of those accomplishments bring you the deepest sense of pride and joy.

Look at your life in other ways, too. Hobbies, for example, can sometimes be stepping stones toward deeper passions and ambitions. If you love to read novels, for example, maybe your dream could be to write a book yourself. This is a great way to find your ambitions, as our hobbies are often things that bring us immense happiness.

Your hobbies might also be remnants of a dream you set aside, as they're a way you could still include that dream in your life. Try to devote some extra time to this hobby, in order to see if that's your case.

Your talents are also a way you can discover your true desires. It's no secret that people enjoy doing what they're good at, and everyone is good at something. Think about the things that came naturally to you, and spend time engaging in those activities. There's a good chance this will spark something within you.

Consider your past, as well as your present, when reflecting on the little things. What moments in your memory brought you happiness? There are probably some moments that stand out to you compared to others, so reflect on those moments to see if you can find the reason why they're so distinct in your memory.

When considering your past happiness, think about what working environments brought you joy. Some people are happiest working with their hands, while others thrive in outdoor environments. Some prefer working with other people, while others prefer to work with animals, or even machines.

It's hard to see yourself clearly, as many different things can cloud your vision. It's also hard to find anyone who has a perfect idea of who they are. That's why it's so important to look around you. Finding the environments, people, and experiences that bring joy to your life is how you can begin to see the shape of yourself.

It's like the concept of negative space in art. Negative space is the area around an object that, in turn, gives shape to the object. It's the space between a mug and its handle, between the focus of the painting and the edges of the canvas. When you look at the area around yourself, the image of your true self will come into focus.

Step Two: Brainstorm

The next step is to try brainstorming. After you've looked inside yourself, try taking a step back and thinking about what you want. Try to visualize yourself in the future, and note what your mind conjures up. Where are you? What are you doing? Who are you with? All of these are questions you should be asking yourself during this time.

There are all kinds of ways you can brainstorm for your future; it's just a matter of finding the best way for you. Some people like to sit back and think, while others prefer to write things down in a journal. You could even make a vision board for yourself and fill it with images you might aspire toward.

Talking to a trusted confidante, like a friend or family member, is also a great way to brainstorm. If you have someone you feel you can talk to, try to get their perspective on your situation. Their insights might surprise you, and even spark new ideas within your mind.

If you aren't sure where to get started when brainstorming, here are a few prompts you can ask yourself, to help get yourself started:

- What brings you joy?

- What would you do if money weren't an issue?

- What qualities do you admire in others?

- What qualities do others admire in you?

- What do you value?

- What do you fear?

You can use these prompts to engage in an easy brainstorming exercise. Take one of these questions, and write it on the top of a piece of paper. Then, set a timer for three to five minutes, and write down every answer that springs to mind. Don't worry about making them reasonable or realistic—this isn't about finding the perfect answer. Instead, this exercise is about getting your brain going, and teaching yourself to think about these topics.

Once your timer goes off, stop writing, and look at the list. There's a good chance that, within all your answers, one will stick out to you the most. Take that answer, and spend a few minutes considering it. Ask yourself why this specific answer stuck out to you compared to the others. There's a good chance that doing this will help you uncover a truth about yourself.

Step Three: Summarize and Analyze

After brainstorming, it's time to dig into the answers you've found. Summarize your thoughts, and analyze what you have discovered. Take the key points you have come up with and expand upon them, boring into them to find the truth at the core.

For example, if you find that the idea of helping others brings you the most joy, and you think that that might be your dream, think about how you might want to go about doing this. In what ways can you help other people? What do you want to help them with?

These questions will help you develop a clear vision of your future goals. Consider what your dream is, and how you see yourself going about this dream. Ask where you are, and who you are with, when engaging in this future. See if there are any tools you need to achieve this goal, or any other external sources of assistance you might require.

As you create this clear vision of your future, you are, in many ways, bringing that future to life through visualization. You envision yourself doing something and, in doing so, convince your mind that you are already doing that thing. This is the power of belief, and it is mighty indeed. Believe in yourself, don't give up, and everything else will, in time, fall into place.

Step Four: Planning

Once you have a clear vision for your future, it's time to plan how to get there! Creating a road map for your success is a great way to make a plan of action for achieving your dreams.

Do as much research as you can when you start your plan. The more you know about a topic, the more straightforward creating your road map will be. After all, the more you know about something, the more you will understand it.

You can also look into finding a mentor during the planning phase. Talking to someone who has achieved your goals can be incredibly beneficial for creating your plan to get there. They could have insights into things you might not have considered before, or tips on making specific steps easier, and avoiding particular obstacles.

When getting down to creating the road map, I'd recommend trying something known as backward planning. Start at your end goal, and then consider what might be the last step required before you reach that destination. Keep working backward from there, until you reach the first step in the process, and then focus your mental energy there.

This is a great way to plan, as I find figuring out where to start is sometimes more difficult than starting! Instead of wondering how you can achieve your goal, you start from the end—from the moment you have already achieved the desired result—and are now simply looking at the process you took to make it there.

Step Five: Live Your Truths

After you've reflected, brainstormed, created a clear vision, and made a plan, it's finally time to take the first step, and start making your journey toward the future of your dreams. Of course, this is easier said than done. It can be hard to consistently stick to the path you've set out for yourself. Life will throw roadblocks and diversions in your way, and it's up to you to keep forging ahead despite all that .

Staying Motivated

Staying motivated is a challenge I'm sure all of us know well. However, it's also one of the most vital parts of achieving your dreams. Think of any time you've heard an interview from someone who has achieved success in their life; someone who has made their dreams come true. They always talk about how they never gave up, even when things got hard. That's the type of drive that can propel you forward.

One great way I've found to remain motivated in this journey is to find a community of like-minded people; others who share your dreams and passions. When you spend time with people who share these interests, you can inspire each other and take strength from each other.

Knowing that other people are there with you on this journey can sometimes make all the difference.

Another way to stay motivated is to set a specific time each week for working toward your dreams. When you schedule this time into your life, making it an event on your calendar, you'll be more likely to follow through on what you need to be doing. Think about times you might have spent scrolling through your phone or binge-watching television. That's time you could be spending working toward your ideal future instead.

Stay flexible and open to making changes to your plan as well! Sometimes those roadblocks that life puts in your path are unavoidable. No one knows what the future holds, and the unexpected will always happen, no matter how hard you try. When something derails your plan, don't try to forge ahead, even when you know it can no longer work. Instead, try to see how you can work these new developments into your plan. Your plans aren't set in stone, after all. If allowing yourself to bend so you don't break is what you need to do, then bend to make your dreams a reality!

Ignoring self-doubt is also essential to continuing to live your truth. It's all too easy to listen to the negative voices in your head; the ones that are constantly criticizing you, and telling you that you aren't good enough. But remember, that negative voice isn't true, and it isn't you! Doubts are poison and, if you let them in, they can crush your spirit and kill your dreams. So, even if other people doubt you, make sure you don't doubt yourself. Remember: You have a plan, you've put in the work, and you are more than capable of doing this.

Having a mantra is also a great way to stay motivated, and it has the bonus of keeping self-doubt at bay. Sometimes, no matter what, you're going to feel demoralized. These days happen to every single person. However, having a mantra to fall back on can help you power through these bad days, and stay on track with your ambitions.

How to Create Your Mantra

When you're having a hard time, don't let it fester. Instead, take that negativity and turn it into something positive. This is how you can create a mantra for your life and goals.

On a day when you feel demoralized and unmotivated regarding your dreams, write down that negative feeling. Then, cross out those words. This is a symbolic act of you letting go and destroying those negative emotions. After this, take those negative words and rewrite that first sentence, turning it into a more positive statement; a truth that reflects your life.

For example, your negative thoughts could be, "it's unrealistic of me to even attempt to achieve these goals." When you rewrite this, you could say something like, "I am more than capable of making my dreams come true" or, "sometimes, taking a risk is the only way to move forward."

Whatever the case, create your mantra by directly challenging and disproving your negative self-talk. Once you have your mantra, say it each day, write it down somewhere visible, and keep it in your mind to use as a shield against your doubts.

These five steps will help guide you toward creating the future you want. All you have to do is put in the work and choose to strive for that future.

Goal Examples to Help Inspire You

Even with the five-step method, you might still struggle to find your goals, which is entirely understandable! It's hard to define your goals in a specific way, as dreams can often feel nebulous and vague. It doesn't help, either, that there seem to be so many categories of dreams! Some people have career dreams, while others dream of travel and adventure. There are some people, too, who want to work on themselves as people. With so many different possible passions and directions you can take, it can be hard to know what to do.

Fortunately, it's easier than you might think to categorize your ambitions, as what you dream for your future will likely fall under the broad category of personal dreams. These dreams are things you want for yourself and your future, which is what this book is about.

The majority of personal goals fall into a few categories: Personal growth and self-development, career, family, and life goals. I'll give examples of what goals fall into each of these categories—and what they look like—so you can take inspiration, and use them as a way to discover your dreams.

Personal Growth and Self-Development Goals

Personal growth goals focus on improving your current self. Things like learning a new language, eating healthier, being more compassionate, embracing creativity, and learning to let go of the past are all examples of goals geared toward your self-development.

Personal Career Goals

Career goals are precisely what they sound like—ambitions centered around your work life. Goals like improving your work-life balance, learning to speak up more in meetings, practicing conflict resolution, and getting a promotion are all great examples of the more career-driven goals.

Of course, career goals aren't just about being better in your current job. Some personal career goals are more geared toward finding a new job, in which case improving your interview skills, learning to network, or learning new skills to make yourself qualified for your dream job are examples of these sorts of goals.

Personal Family Goals

Family goals involve putting the work in to improve your home life and your relationship with your family. Prioritizing family time might be one of these goals, as is learning new communication strategies to better relate to your family members.

Family goals can also be fun! Maybe you want to plan a family vacation, or you want to find fun ways to spend time together as a family. Both of these are excellent examples of personal goals relating to your family.

Personal Life Goals

Personal life goals are similar to personal growth goals. While this overlap exists, the key difference is that personal life goals involve making changes to your quality of life rather than how you move through life.

Learning how to manage stress is a life goal that you might also consider a growth goal. However, working toward financial stability is pretty clearly a life goal rather than a growth goal.

Life goals aren't just about changing the quality of your life. They also include things that you want to do in your life.

Think of plans for traveling, or trying exciting experiences that push you out of your comfort zone, like skydiving. These are both great examples of personal life goals you can set.

Looking at these examples of different goals, it's easy to see that the options for your life's path are limitless. Remember as well, though, that you don't have to pick just one goal! If your overall goal is to land your dream goal, then setting smaller goals that can act as milestones to help you, like learning new skills and gaining qualifications, is an excellent method to achieving success.

You don't even have to make your goals related. If your dream is to find ways to be more creative in life and also travel more, that's amazing! These goals might not be intertwined, but nothing is stopping you from achieving both things. Besides, you might find your dreams connecting in unexpected ways. If, like me, you love art, then both taking up painting as a hobby and traveling to famous galleries around the world can help fulfill that passion in your life.

Take inspiration from these goals, and use them to start envisioning your future. Once you do this, you'll be ready to use the five steps framework of realizing your dreams to begin to set your goals and achieve your ambitions.

Chapter 4

Planning

Make Meaningful Change

"A goal properly set is halfway reached."

—Zig Ziglar

I don't have a linear mind. In fact, sometimes it seems to me that I have a mass of tangled thoughts in my head. I am easily distracted, I forget things, I get enthusiastic—before soon enough losing my motivation—and in short, I am a hopeless case.

Planning is not easy, but it is absolutely essential for me, as it prevents me from getting lost in the labyrinth of my mind. To plan, I need to set a goal, and I need to decide on the steps to take to achieve that goal.

It seems like a straightforward process, setting goals. You decide what you want to pursue, figure out the path to reach that goal, and then get started. But what happens when, even with this plan, everything falls apart? To have set your goals, and then find that the path you chose to reach them isn't leading you in the right direction, is incredibly demoralizing. When you lose your way like that, it's hard to double back, see where you made a wrong turn, and restart your journey.

It doesn't have to be like that, though. With a bit of planning, understanding, and proper goal setting, you can make sure your path forward runs smoothly. I'll take you through the reasons you absolutely should take the time to ensure you have adequately planned your goals, and how to partake in SMART goal setting—that is, creating Specific, Measurable, Achievable, Relevant, and Time-bound goals. By the time we're through, you'll see the incredible benefits of proper goal setting, and you'll also be one step closer to setting goals for yourself.

The Key to Success: Goal Setting

Goal setting is more than simply stating a goal aloud. As I mentioned previously, it's about creating a workable plan of action—think of step four of the five-step method for understanding yourself. While deciding on the goal itself is vital, the planning phase is just as—if not more—vital.

Despite this importance, it's easy to forget how critical it is to set goals. I think, for many people, there's a tendency to get stuck in the planning phase of any process. It's hard to create a map to lead you somewhere you haven't been before. However, setting goals is about more than planning for the future. Looking at its other undeniable benefits, you might see a more straightforward way ahead.

Goal setting is, in many ways, about gaining mastery over yourself. It's about learning how to have focus, and keep that focus up as you continue ahead. When you set goals, you learn to believe in yourself, thereby promoting your self-efficacy and, in many ways, turning a dream into a self-fulfilling prophecy. You think you can achieve the goal, and so you do.

Studies have been conducted on the self-efficacy that is born from setting goals. One such study looked at athletes in rehabilitation programs after sustaining an injury. It found that the groups who set and followed a plan of action were the ones more likely to believe in themselves and their recovery and, as such, were more motivated and less demoralized regarding their recuperation (Evans & Hardy, 2002).

When you set goals, you stoke the flames of motivation within your heart. With a strong plan, you can keep that flame of motivation burning within you, despite any winds or rains you might encounter on your journey.

There are so many benefits to setting goals. During my time working toward my dreams, I've experienced these benefits and, as such, have put together a few of them, so that you can see some of the incredible things goal setting can do for you.

Provides Direction

Goals give you direction in life. Have you ever found that, after giving up on some of your dreams, you seemed to move with the currents of life? While there's nothing wrong with 'going with the flow' occasionally, it isn't a sustainable way to live. Eventually, those currents will get you lost if you don't do something about them.

On the other hand, goals will point you in the right direction. They are your compass and your North Star, telling you where you need to go. When you set a lifetime goal, you can focus your energy and efforts on a specific place, and make meaningful decisions to reach that destination.

Grants Clarity

Setting goals can also help you gain clarity. You will better understand what you value and desire not only out of life, but for yourself, and you will also be more equipped to make quick decisions.

When you lack focus in life, you're more likely to be indecisive. After all, how can you choose which path is best to take without knowing where you're going? With goals, you will be able to make wise and quick decisions that will guide you toward the life you desire.

Gives You Control

Having set goals will grant you control over your life. When you decide on a dream you wish to pursue, you are taking the reins of your life into your hands, and controlling where you go.

Writing down your goals and making a plan helps you see your future unfurling before you. This clarity of vision grants you the strength and knowledge to know the shape you would like your life to take, and the power to ensure that that dream becomes a reality.

This control is something so many of us long for. After all, feeling like we have no control over our lives is something everyone has experienced at least once. While we might not be able to control the outside forces life exerts upon us, we can still control ourselves and, as such, the future.

Provides Motivation

Goals, as I said, provide incredible motivation. They give you something to aspire to, creating hope within your heart. Hope is, in many ways, one of the strongest forces in the world. So many people have done incredible things based solely on the hope that these things might come true.

By setting goals, you can harness that hope, and use it as a driving force in your life. This force of hope is something you can use to keep and sustain the momentum you need in life when you have a dream.

Grants a Sense of Personal Satisfaction

Goal setting is also remarkably satisfying on a personal level. Think of a time when you have set and achieved a goal, even a relatively small goal. There's a good chance you felt buoyant, nearly triumphant, with the satisfaction of seeing your efforts pay off and result in the conclusion you wanted.

Think about the satisfaction that will follow another dream, perhaps a larger one. When you work toward a vision, you can see your potential in action. This helps you recognize the strengths that already exist within you, which are often easy to overlook. By understanding your capabilities, you gain a sense of pride and appreciation for who you are, and what you can achieve.

Provides Purpose

Setting goals will also provide a sense of purpose in your life. This purpose is similar to direction, but it's more than that. While direction feeds into motivation and clarity of vision, showing you the way forward, having a purpose in life is more all-encompassing.

When you gain purpose in life, you gain a reason to live, and you keep living in strength, happiness, and joy. If you're reading this and thinking that you might have already found purpose in life, remember that your life can have more than one purpose.

After all, having purpose is about more than a single goal. It's about understanding who you are, and what you were meant to do with your life. It's about knowing yourself, and this self-knowledge includes gaining a sense of what you already have, and what else you would like to include in your life.

For some people, gaining a purpose can make all the difference. It can be what gets you out of bed some mornings. Your purpose is about learning and celebrating who you are, and everything that goes along with that. When you create goals that complement this purpose, that coincide with the reality of you, your life gains deeper meaning.

———————◆○◆———————

Everything You Need to Know About SMART Goals

Knowing, yourself, some of the benefits of setting goals, you might wonder why so many people don't achieve the goals they set. Take New Year's resolutions, for example. Have you ever set one and, despite every intention you might have had to make that resolution a reality, forgot about it a few months into the year?

Even with a plan, and even with the best intentions, your goals might not be achievable. Sometimes, even when you do your best to stick to your goals, they might not be something you can reach. This is why you should look at the goals themselves, as they form the foundation for your goal setting.

What Are SMART Goals?

When you decide on your goal, it's essential to make sure it's a SMART goal. As I mentioned, SMART is an acronym that stands for specific, measurable, achievable, relevant, and time-bound.

Making a goal like "I want to exercise more" isn't inherently wrong. However, it is vague, and in that ambiguity, problems begin to arise. Using the SMART formula, you would create a goal that would sound something like, "I want to run a marathon by the end of the coming year."

That specificity defines your goal, and lays the groundwork for creating a plan of action. With those parameters set, you can determine things like an achievable exercise plan, as well as smaller goals that you can use to measure your progress, such as five or ten kilometer runs, or running a half-marathon.

When you're setting a SMART goal, go through each of the letters in the acronym and use them to help you create a plan that will work for you, and not against you.

Specific

Being specific with what you want to accomplish helps you with your focus. After all, it's easy to become distracted by other things when you have only a broad idea of what you would like to see in your future. Having specificity creates a clarity of purpose and narrows your focus, so you can keep on track with your goal.

This narrower vision helps with planning. Take the marathon goal, for example. Rather than the vague idea of exercising more, you have a specific goal of running a marathon. You can research preparing for marathons, and reach out to other runners. You can even find running groups to join, in order to find a community that shares your interests.

Measurable

Ensuring that your goal is something you can measure is vital for its success. Being able to measure your goal means you can track your progress and see how much you can improve and accomplish to achieve your ultimate dream.

Measuring your progress can be done in a lot of ways. For goals like the marathon example, it's easy to measure and create milestones you can use to keep track of where you are on your journey.

However, it can be more challenging for other goals to find a specific measure. If you want to be more compassionate, it's hard to know how to look inward, and see where you stand with your progress. In those cases, try to keep a journal, and write down your mindset during different times, and how you handled these various situations. You'll be able to look back on that journal, and see how your reactions have evolved.

Achievable

A big part of setting a goal is ensuring that it isn't an impossible task. You want to have a goal you can conceivably reach. Otherwise, you're setting yourself up for failure. Goals like winning the lottery aren't something that you will ever be able to have any control over and, as such, aren't goals at all.

Additionally, it's all too common for people to set huge goals, and believe that having a grandiose dream is motivating. However, with unattainable dreams, you're only going to feel demoralized and disappointed.

This isn't to say that you shouldn't have big dreams, because you absolutely should! That being said, you should consider time, skill, and other external factors that might affect your goal.

For example, take the dream of becoming the CEO of a company. This goal will take time, especially if you're just starting your career. If you set a goal of becoming CEO in two years, there's a good chance you won't achieve it, unless you're already one promotion away from that role.

Instead, set more achievable goals. Look at the career track of a CEO, and set goals for reaching certain positions within time frames, gaining the qualifications needed for the ultimate role along the way, and networking goals to help you gain connections for your journey. This way, you'll be steadily making progress and getting yourself into the best possible position for accomplishing the larger goal. In time, you'll find that becoming the CEO is entirely attainable.

Creating achievable goals isn't about "being realistic" and giving up on your big dreams. It's about understanding the world around you and how its limitations can play a role in the timeline of your goals. After all, your goals should depend on you, and what you can achieve—not anyone or anything else.

Relevant

Make sure your goals are relevant to your life and who you are. This is why it's important to look inward and understand your values and desires. After all, if your goal doesn't align with your true values and wants when it comes to your life and future, it isn't going to be something you'll want to achieve in the long-term.

Understanding what you need in life and what brings you happiness and fulfillment will help you make goals that matter to you. When making a goal, ask yourself why it is important to you, and how achieving this goal will help you. If you don't have a good answer to these questions, there's a good chance the goal isn't relevant to your life.

Time-Bound

Finally, try to set goals that exist within a time frame. Having a realistic deadline for your plan will help you stay motivated throughout the process, and lend additional weight to the feeling that you are working toward something.

It also helps you have a set finish line for your goal, especially with personal self-development goals. Learning how to manage stress in your life is a good thing to do, but it's also something of a life-long commitment. Setting smaller goals within specific timelines, such as mastering various stress management techniques within a few months, will help you work toward the larger goal, while keeping you on track with your progress.

Ask yourself what you can accomplish each day to work toward your goal. Then ask what you can achieve in a week, a month, or six months. This will help you determine the correct time frame for your goal, so that your end date is reasonable in both directions. You don't want a time frame that's too short, as that will lead to stress, and you also don't want a time frame that's too long, as that leads to a lack of motivation, and the potential for procrastination.

Two Steps to Setting Personal Goals

In the example of being a CEO, you might have noticed that I mentioned taking the larger goal, and focusing your efforts on achieving other goals in the interim. Taking a significant goal—one that you might refer to as a lifetime goal—and breaking it down into various smaller goals, is a great way to make those seemingly larger-than-life dreams come true. These two steps are the key to setting personal goals that will work for you.

Step One: Setting Lifetime Goals

When it comes to setting a lifetime goal, you will need to take a step back and look at your situation with a little bit of distance. Having a broad perspective so you can take in all aspects of your life will help you determine what you want overall.

Knowing this lifetime goal can help you gain perspective on the smaller goals you might want to accomplish in life. It can also help shape your decision-making, as you will know your ultimate destination. Any decisions you make will be helped by the knowledge of where you're eventually headed.

Consider different aspects of your life, and see if any lifetime goals ring particularly true when you turn your attention to these aspects. Remember, you can have more than one lifetime goal, and they don't necessarily have to be connected. Humans have so many layers and interests and wants and needs, that it's impossible to find any singular goal that will entirely define their existence.

Here are a few of the categories of your life wherein you might consider developing a lifetime goal:

Career

As always, career goals are pretty standard, and this is because your career can become a massive part of your life and identity. Think about the career you have, and the career you might want to have. Is there a specific field, job, or position you're interested in pursuing?

I mentioned the goal of becoming a CEO, but there's more to a career than business. Maybe you want to be involved in scientific research, or you want to become a professional singer. Whatever the case, career goals can make excellent lifetime goals.

Finances

Financial goals are another big one that can drive your life. When I discussed finances, I showed how you could work toward financial freedom. For some people, financial freedom is a stepping stone toward another dream. For others, though, financial freedom is the ultimate lifetime dream.

Education

Education goals can be a lifelong pursuit. It's an intrinsic quality to humanity, the desire to learn constantly. We're curious by nature, and that curiosity drives us to achieve incredible things.

Maybe you never finished your education, and want to go back to school. Perhaps you already have multiple degrees, but you still want to learn more. Maybe your education dreams aren't specific to traditional education, but are instead geared toward learning a new skill outside of schooling.

Whatever the case, ask yourself if there's any specific knowledge you wish to learn, or if there's any knowledge that can help you achieve different dreams. In either case, focusing some of your goals on education is a good idea.

Family

For some of us, the greatest dream is to start a family. We want to be good parents and good partners, so we focus our efforts on this area of our lives. If you already have a family, consider other dreams that coincide with this aspect of your life. After all, you never stop being a parent. Maybe your lifelong dream is to always be there with love and support for your family.

Mindset

Lifelong dreams might be about internal growth. These are the types of self-development dreams I discussed previously. If you've been through hardships in life you're struggling to move past, you might want to set a goal of moving on from the past and adopting a different attitude toward life.

Even if you haven't experienced anything like that, you might still want to work toward being a changed person. After all, we're never done growing in life, and there's always room for us to evolve. We all have specific behavioral patterns we might like to change, so striving to make that change counts as a lifetime goal.

Creative

Finding ways to be creative and achieve artistic goals is another critical area of your life, and is an excellent way to find lifetime goals you might not have considered. Maybe you want to paint a portrait of a loved one, or write a book of poetry. Whatever the case, working toward these artistic goals is a beautiful thing.

Physical

Working on your health and well-being is absolutely a lifetime goal. Healthy living, after all, sometimes means adopting an entirely new lifestyle. Eating healthy, exercising more, and other athletic and health-related goals fall under this category.

Enjoyment

Personal enjoyment can be a treasure trove of lifetime goals. Finding ways to love your life and enjoy your time here on Earth is just as important as any other type of goal. After all, happiness begets happiness. If your goal is to foster joy in your life, that joy will radiate from you and find its way into the lives of others.

Remember that these categories aren't the only ones. There might be all kinds of areas of your life you could draw upon to uncover lifetime goals. Just make sure that the goals you settle on are what you want to achieve, not what anyone else makes you think you want.

Step Two: Setting Smaller Goals

Once you have your lifetime goals decided, consider how to distill those goals. This is where SMART goals often come into play. Use the SMART roadmap to develop and refine these goals until you have a clear plan of action for how to move forward in life.

Ask yourself what you need to achieve to reach your larger goal. Using the idea of running a marathon, set smaller goals for completing other runs, like the 5k, or a half-marathon.

When you set these smaller goals, ask yourself when it would be reasonable for you to achieve them, and include them on your overall timeline. For lifetime goals like becoming a CEO, work backward and create a ten-year, five-year, one-year, and six-month plan. Make a note of what qualifications or certifications you might need by what time, and factor that into your goal.

When you have your smaller goals set, do another check, and make sure your plans are in line with how you want to live. If you haven't factored in room for other goals or things that bring you happiness, you might want to revise your roadmap. After all, the occasional detour can be an excellent thing.

Ten Tips to Help You on Your Journey

When it comes to setting goals, you can do a few things to help refine and define what it is that you truly desire. While

I can tell you to look inside yourself and make five-year plans, you might still be asking how. Not everyone is good at planning, and, even if you are, a few extra tips can be beneficial. Here are ten tips I've learned from my time setting goals, and planning for the future:

Pursue Your Passions

It's easier to achieve your goals when pursuing something that matters to you. There are, inevitably, things that we have to do in life that we don't necessarily care about. When it comes to your dreams, you want to ensure that you're chasing after what you love.

Life is meant to be enjoyed. I believe that wholeheartedly, and I encourage you to adopt that mindset. If you aren't filling your life with what you love, then the loveless things in your life aren't going to push you or motivate you. Instead, they'll hold you back and keep you down.

Find what makes you happy, and pursue that passion with all your heart. Don't think about society, life, the opinions of others, or any other external factors. Focus your attention on what creates joy in your life, and find a way you can turn that into a goal for your future. If you're passionate about your dreams, you will be more motivated to make them a reality.

Find Your Why

When you feel overwhelmed, as you try to determine what your goals should be, or which goals you should pursue at what time, you will likely need to take a step back and think a few things over. If you feel stretched thin and exhausted by the idea of setting goals, you should ask yourself why you're doing this in the first place.

Reconnecting with your original desire, need, or other driving force will help you regain focus and remember why you are doing this in the first place. Remember, these are goals for you and your future. Be honest with yourself about why these goals matter to you.

Dive Deep

The more time and effort you put into planning your goals, the more likely you are to accomplish them. When things are done on a whim, it's just as easy to quit as it was to begin impulsively. However, putting in genuine hard work, and being honest with yourself, will help you create goals that you can stick with for the long run.

Trust Your Gut

Sometimes you see what your friends, family, or other people are doing, and you convince yourself that that's what you want. While that can sometimes be true, it's also true that what's best for other people won't always be what is best for you.

Look to others for advice or inspiration, but remember that the decision you make regarding the direction you take your future is up to you, and you alone. Listen to your instincts when you try new things.

Pay attention to how you feel, and consider those feelings. More often than not, you already know what you truly want and need. You just have to trust in yourself, and take the time to listen.

Commit

If you want to achieve your dreams, you will have to make a commitment. If you think you aren't ready to commit to certain things at this time, plan to get started on your goal once you have the time or energy, rather than trying to make it happen anyway.

Getting into a place where you are ready to commit to pursuing your dreams is, in my opinion, an important part of goal setting. So if you feel like you can't commit right now, take your time, and when you're ready and able, you can start this journey. However, be careful not to procrastinate too much. Postponing because we don't feel ready is an easy excuse not to start; to delay what we are afraid to face. For that reason, always keep these words in mind: "If not now, when?"

Write Down Your Goals

Sometimes writing something down can make it seem real. I think it has to do with the tangibility of it; the act of putting pen to paper and seeing the words form, then holding that paper in your hand. These little things remind you that this is something you want, and that this is a dream that is real, and lives inside you.

When I chose to pursue my dreams, writing them down brought me intense relief. There they were, those dreams I had held in my heart for so long, no longer just living in my head, but instead existing in the world. It felt real at that moment, and it strengthened my resolve to continue down this path toward creating a future filled with more and more happiness.

Having your goals written down and kept somewhere visible also serves as a reminder of what you're working toward. It can keep you motivated and on track as you forge ahead.

Stay Positive

While it's impossible to be positive all the time, it's also important not to use that as an excuse to engage in self-doubt and negativity. We all have bad days, but you don't have to let those days define you.

Remember to believe in yourself and your ability to make your dreams come true. Remember why you are doing this, and remind yourself of the future you are working toward, as you do your best to keep a positive attitude.

Try to engage in positive acts each day to keep you motivated. This can be a more significant thing, like something that genuinely propels you forward with your goal, or it can be something smaller, such as telling a friend about your dreams. These positive actions will help keep you from getting too down in the dumps when those bad days rear their heads.

Learn From Failures

When those bad days do come, or you fall short of reaching a milestone or accomplishing something you wanted, don't give in to negativity. Rather than being defeated by failures, take them as a learning opportunity.

After all, a failure isn't an ending. Just because something didn't work out once doesn't mean it never will. Pick yourself back up and try again, taking the lessons from that failure, and using them to achieve success next time.

Prioritize One Goal at a Time

If you have multiple goals, it's essential to know which plan will have the top priority. If you're trying to split your focus equally between several goals, you'll feel burned out. By having one goal as your main priority, you can focus your energy there, and ensure that you give that task your best work and effort.

Daily Planning

Another powerful tool to help you set your goals and work toward your dreams is daily planning. Time gets away from all of us. If you don't have a good time management strategy, you might look back as you pull up the covers in the evening, and wonder what you did all day.

Especially after breaks in your routine, like holidays and vacations, getting back on track and refocusing on what you need to accomplish is challenging. While breaking our routines is a good thing, as it can refresh our minds and renew our motivation, it's also hard to get back into things. When the holiday is over, it's like we need a guideline to help us start over.

Daily planning acts as that guideline, helping you effectively manage your time to achieve all you need to on that day. It reduces stress, as it helps you construct a clear picture of what your day will look like. This plan of action is a great way to get organized and move forward on your journey.

There are a few different ways to plan your day, but I have a few tips. Writing your plan down, for example, is a great way to organize your thoughts and determine which tasks you should prioritize. Not only that, but writing down your schedule means you don't have to constantly try to remember when you were going to do each thing, as you'll have it right there in front of you.

When making your plan, be sure to include a split between work and life tasks. After all, finding a healthy work-life balance is essential for keeping yourself motivated and focused on your tasks.

However, I would say the key to daily planning is weekly planning. Weekly planning entails coming up with a master plan of what you would like to accomplish that week. Once you've determined these broader strokes, you can then break your week down, day by day, to come up with a schedule that will keep you on track to accomplish your weekly goals.

When I plan out my week and days like this, I typically like to do so in the morning, when my mind is fresh. However, planning the night before works as well.

I begin my planning session by brainstorming and writing down all I need to get done that day, dividing them into work and personal tasks. Then I prioritize my tasks into what is urgent and what is not. As I complete each task, I draw a line through it as a visual representation of what I have accomplished, and what I still need to get done.

You can include this in your plan when creating your daily schedule. Set aside a block of time each morning for this planning process. It's a way to start your morning off right, as you will have accomplished these three elements of creating a schedule: Brainstorming, dividing, and prioritizing.

It is helpful to include operations that require little time in the list as well. These smaller tasks give us the feeling of having done more things. If there were only larger tasks that take a lot of time to complete, we would feel that we have done little.

Time Blocking

One of the biggest problems people face when planning their day is achieving that elusive balance. Including both big and small tasks is one of the ways to make your schedule more balanced, but sometimes even that can be overwhelming. This is where a planning technique known as time blocking can make your life easier.

Time blocking is a time management strategy where you break your entire day up into blocks of time. You fill these blocks with what you need to accomplish, and, during that time, you focus solely on the task at hand.

This technique is a great way to stay focused, as it operates on the idea of eliminating multi-tasking. Rather than splitting your attention between several things, you devote all your focus to the one task ahead of you. You will be more likely to complete the task at hand, and you'll have made sure that it entailed all your best efforts.

You can include several smaller tasks during your block of time, like checking and answering your emails in the morning. This is known as task batching, wherein you group several similar smaller tasks into one block of time.

When planning your day, look at everything you need to get done. You can begin to split your day into blocks, and fill those blocks with your tasks. Remember to schedule time for breaks as well, though. It's easy to fill your day with only work, but a day like that isn't going to be productive in the long run. Taking breaks and spending time doing things you enjoy boosts your motivation, rather than taking away from it.

The Eisenhower Matrix

The Eisenhower Matrix is a tool you can use to help prioritize your tasks. It's an excellent method to use in conjunction with time blocking, as it is a tool that you can use to prioritize your daily tasks depending on their importance and urgency.

When you have your list of what you need to accomplish during the day, draw a four-square grid on a piece of paper. The squares are as follows: do, schedule, delegate, and delete. Using the concepts of urgent, not-urgent, important, and not-important, you'll be able to divide your tasks into the four squares you've set up.

The first square, for the tasks you need to do, is intended for projects that are both urgent and important. These are the tasks you absolutely need to prioritize and get done that day.

The second square is for the tasks you need to schedule. That is, tasks that are important, but not urgent. While essential for long-term goals, these are tasks that don't need to be completed immediately, and can be scheduled for later if need be.

Tasks you can delegate go in the third square. These tasks are urgent, but not important. If you were a boss, these are the tasks you could delegate to your employees. While they need to be done now, these are quick tasks that aren't as important to your long-term goals. Think of things like answering emails or phone calls; they need to get done, but they aren't a crucial part of accomplishing your goals.

Finally, there's the fourth square. This is where you put your tasks you can delete, as they're neither urgent nor important. These are the distractions you might typically indulge in during the day as a way to procrastinate.

When you use this prioritization technique in conjunction with time blocking, you'll be able to block off the time you need for each project more accurately. This makes it easier for you to plan your day, in order to help you move your goals forward.

The Pomodoro Technique

Let's say, while creating your daily plan, you set aside a two-hour block of time to work on a larger project. On the one hand, this is great because you're making space for this task in your schedule. On the other hand, it's hard for people to focus for two hours straight.

This is where the Pomodoro technique can help. This technique is a great way to break down these larger blocks of time, and keep you focused on your work without becoming overwhelmed.

The Pomodoro technique is brilliant in its simplicity. When you start working, set a timer for 25 minutes and work without distractions for the entirety of those 25-minute sessions. When your timer goes off, take a five-minute break. When the break is up, set another 25-minute timer and get back to work. Once you've completed four of these sessions, take an extended break, around 15-30 minutes.

After each session, mark off that session and record what you accomplished. At the end of your four sessions, you'll be able to see all the progress you made during that time.

This technique is a great way to combat distractions and be productive. You can incorporate it into your other daily planning techniques, like time blocking, or use it to drive your entire daily plan.

When planning your day, you might need to experiment with a few different methods. Just as everyone learns differently, we all focus and work differently. Whatever daily planning method you ultimately decide upon, you'll find that scheduling your day will significantly improve your productivity and help you work toward reaching your goals.

———————◄◆►———————

Start Shaping Your Future

It might take some practice to determine how best to create SMART goals. You might find yourself working toward a goal you later decide isn't for you, and that's okay!

Goal setting isn't about immediately knowing the perfect goal for your life. It's about learning who you are, what matters to you, and, in time, what you need to do to achieve those dreams.

I have provided you with a SMART goal template that you can use to help create and set goals that will work for you. You can download it by following the link at the end.

You can use this template to help you ask yourself questions to determine what your goals are. This process will work for significant lifetime goals, as well as mid-term and short-term goals.

If you want to create it yourself, here are the questions I suggest:

- **Specific**
  What do you want to achieve?
  Why do you want this?
  How will you achieve this goal?

- **Measurable**
  How will you know when you have achieved your goal?
  How will you measure your progress?

- **Achievable**
  Do I have what I need to achieve my goal?
  What do I need that I do not have?
  What are some smaller goals that will help me achieve my lifetime goal?

- **Relevant**
  Why is this goal significant to me?
  Does this goal align with my values?
  How will achieving this goal help me?

- **Time-Bound**
  How long will I need to accomplish this goal?
  What is my five-year plan?
  One-year plan?
  Six-month plan?

Remember that this is only one step in the process, so don't get too hung up over creating the perfect goal. Life throws wrenches into plans, no matter how much effort you've put into that plan. This is, ultimately, a guideline rather than a rigid set of rules you must follow. Trust in your abilities and believe in yourself as you move through this process, as that inner faith will be what carries you through life, and into the future.

Chapter 5

Pillars

Create Positive Habits

"Do the best you can, until you know better. Then when you know better, do better."

—Maya Angelou

I don't know about you, but I need to have some sort of routine in my day. Being in the confines of a daily routine feels, to me, like being in a safe place. Maintaining habits allows me to give space to my creativity, and not feel suffocated by uncertainty. Above all, keeping up with routines and habits allows me to proceed with more lightness on my path. They are like pillars that support my day, granting me the freedom to play around with my creativity, while they hold my world in place.

You can set your goals, have all the motivation in the world, and be committed to the task of working hard and reaching for your dreams. However, all of that hard work will be doubled without engaging in good practices and healthy, positive habits to bolster your well-being.

When you have positive habits, you put yourself first. It's the idea of taking care of yourself, in order to ultimately take care of others. No matter your determination, if you don't foster good habits in your life, you won't be able to expend all your best efforts and energies toward achieving your goals.

There's a power that comes from fostering positive habits, and it's the power that lives alongside creating positive change and setting yourself up for success. With healthy habits, you can reach inside yourself, bring forth your truest potential, and grow in new, positive directions in every sphere of your life.

When it comes to achieving your goals, there's no tool more powerful you can have in your arsenal than positive habits. These habits will form the backbone of your efforts and help carry you through each phase of your life plans.

Positive habits can make all the difference between achieving your goals and giving up on them. A study conducted in 2007 examined the relationship between positive habits and goal setting. This study found a deep and reciprocal connection between our habits and our goals, and that if you have healthy habits reinforcing your goal-oriented mindset, you will be more able to achieve what you set out to do. Not only that, but this study found that we're also more likely to achieve success faster when we engage in positive behaviors (Wood & Neal, 2007).

The idea that the process of reaching your dreams can be quickened by engaging in positive daily habits is incredible. Don't think that it's overwhelmingly challenging either—healthy habits are more than things you should implement in your life. They're also behaviors that are easy to include in your routines.

I mentioned before how important it is to stay motivated, and offered a few ways you can maintain your determination. Many of those tips are examples of positive habits you can start to use in your day-to-day activities. Reflect on your current practices, and see whether they're helping or hurting you and your progress.

As you move through this chapter, keep thinking about your daily routines. You probably already engage in several healthy habits, just as you might engage in some unhealthy ones. Consider why you partake in those behaviors, and how they affect your life differently. Why do some of your habits help you? Why do others not? Figuring out which behaviors suit your lifestyle and needs will better help you determine how to incorporate positive change into your life.

<hr/>

How to Build Positive Habits

Since habits are an unconscious process, it can be hard to determine precisely how you formed the habits you already have. While some habits are easy enough to determine the origin of—brushing your teeth, for example, is a habit typically created in childhood—others are trickier to pin down.

Think about habits you do have. What prompts you to engage in them? Often, habits are a response to the mechanisms in your brain centered around seeking out and responding to rewards. When you experience a particular trigger—smells, emotions, and sounds are some examples of stimulus triggers—your brain is conditioned to react in specific ways.

The great thing about this is that, through practice, we can train our brains into responding to these triggers the way we want. For example, when you feel stressed out, you might be in the habit of overthinking, smoking, biting your nails, or other unhealthy habits.

However, you can replace these patterns with healthier ones, like going for a walk or taking deep breaths. In time, your brain will begin to respond to your stress with those healthy behaviors, rather than the harmful ones.

The Habit Loop

The process of forming habits doesn't go away as soon as you start to engage in positive behaviors. Instead, it's a constant cycle; an ever-present loop playing over and over unconsciously in our minds. This cycle is known as the habit loop, and it comes in four phases. These phases follow the same pattern for each habit every time you engage in that habit. These phases are the trigger, craving, response, and reward phases.

Trigger

This phase is the initial phase, and it's the one I touched on previously. Our brains are designed to seek out rewards, and, as such, when we encounter a stimulus—or trigger—that our brains know leads to an eventual reward, our brains cue into that trigger, and kickstart the habit l oop.

Craving

The craving phase entails the motivation behind our habits. This phase is what provides a reason to act in the first place.

Remember that it isn't the action that we crave, but instead, it's the reward accompanying that action.

Take brushing your teeth, for example. You wake up in the morning, and you brush your teeth. Once you do so, your mouth feels fresh, your teeth feel clean, and you feel better. It's those feelings of satisfaction that your brain craves, and it's that feeling that drives you to engage in that habit.

Response

The response phase is the action phase. It's when you perform the habit itself. It's the act of brushing your teeth, putting on your seatbelt, or biting your nails. This is a crucial phase when you're seeking to form new habits, as your behavior is dependent on your motivation and willingness to act. If your response to the trigger is too complex, you're less likely to engage in that response.

Reward

Finally, there's the reward phase. This is the end goal; the desired effect of your habit. It's the feeling of satisfaction and cleanliness after brushing your teeth, of anxiety lessening after drinking a glass of wine. This is the result your brain has been waiting for from the moment it began the habit loop.

You should know that rewards aren't just about satisfying cravings. The reward phase is also about teaching your brain which actions you should remember to perform in the future. This second aspect is what you should hone in on when creating new habits in your life. By teaching your brain to remember positive behaviors, you can, slowly but surely, turn them into second nature.

How Long Does It Take to Form a Habit?

You might, at this point, be asking yourself how long it takes for these behaviors to become habits. After all, it's hard to keep reminding yourself to work at something, especially when you have an already ingrained unconscious response.

A common myth claims that it takes 21 days for a behavior to become automatic. However, the reality is that it varies, depending on the person and the behavior. A 2009 study found quite an extensive range for the length of time it takes to form a habit. Their studies found that the range was between 18 and 254 days. On average, however, they found a new habit is formed in about 66 days, or around two months of time (Lally et al., 2009).

The reason for such a large range is that different habits require different exertion levels. Like I said in the response phase of the habit loop, more complex behaviors take more effort, will-power, and determination for someone to consistently include them in their life.

Take morning habits, for example. Getting into the habit of drinking a glass of water before your first cup of morning coffee doesn't take all that much effort. However, engaging in a morning workout routine after having a cup of coffee is significantly more effort and, as such, will take longer to become routine.

Five Mistakes That Keep You From Changing Your Habits

Another reason changing your habits or incorporating new ones might take longer has to do with common mistakes that so often accompany this task. In fact, it isn't only about the difficulty of the task, or your motivation levels. Other factors can influence your ability to change your habits.

Here are five common mistakes people make when trying to make these changes:

Not Controlling Your Environment

If you're trying to eat healthier but constantly go to fast-food restaurants, you'll have a tough time making that change in your life. When you're trying to create positive habits, your environment matters. Remove yourself from situations where you'll be tempted to backslide into old, unhealthy patterns. When you create a healthy environment that supports the change you want to foster within yourself, you'll be more likely to make that change a reality.

Changing Too Many Habits at Once

Sometimes, when we embark on these significant life changes, we get overexcited and try to take on too much at once. It's hard to hold back when you're excited and enthusiastic about the future potential, but sometimes holding back is what you have to do to succeed.

Taking on too much at once leaves you stressed, exhausted, and burned out. That's why you must focus on one habit at a time. Once you have one habit down, you can move on to the next. Until then, though, focus your energies on one t ask.

You Aren't Committed to Change

A habit needing about eight months to stick sounds daunting. It's easier to think that you're going to create these new, healthy habits when you assume they'll only take around three weeks to become automatic. The longer the process takes, the harder it is to stick with your resolve.

If you aren't committed to making this change, you'll be more likely to give up at some point in the process. So, if a habit takes longer than you expected to form, remember to be patient and trust in yourself. You can do it, even if it takes 254 days.

Too Much Emphasis on the Outcome

When you place too much emphasis on the destination, you forget about the journey. Focusing only on the outcome blinds you to the real reason you're trying to make these changes in the first place. Rather than obsessing over short-term goals, remember that forming these new habits is about creating a more positive lifestyle that will outlast any interim goals you set for yourself.

Too Much Focus on the Big Picture

So often, we forget to pay attention to the subtle and gradual changes that these new habits bring about in our lives because we're so focused on the big picture of what our life will look like, once we master these new habits. Instead of focusing on drastic changes you think you need to make in your life, focus your efforts on more minor, more manageable changes that will, over time, add up to a total overhaul of your life and routines.

Seven Steps to Building New Habits

Now that you know what to avoid, the next step is to understand how to start building your new habits. For many of us, creating new habits isn't necessarily about starting from scratch, but instead involves replacing old, unhealthy habits with new, positive ones. With that in mind, here are seven steps you can employ to build healthy habits in your life:

PLAN A FUTURE THAT SETS YOU FREE

Eliminate Your Triggers

If you can figure out the trigger for your bad habits, it's easier to figure out how to control those triggers or eliminate them. After all, if you never enter into the first phase of the habit loop, you won't engage in the unhealthy habit.

Take the time to reflect on your triggers. If there are certain people, places, songs, or other cues that precede your bad habits, try to come up with some strategies to manage those triggers. If you're trying to quit smoking, for example, and you join a friend for a smoke break every time they take one, find a different way you can hang out with that friend—one that doesn't involve smoking.

Stress, as well, is one of the biggest triggers for unhealthy behaviors. Learning to manage your stress levels will significantly help you eliminate the urge to engage in bad habits in the first place.

Reduce Your Cravings

Since your cravings reflect an emotion you want to experience, finding other ways to gain that emotion is a way to change your habits. Figuring out what you're craving, and then determining a healthier way to satiate that craving, is essential for replacing your bad habits with good ones.

After all, these emotions don't have to be achieved through unhealthy methods. If you're trying to cut down on drinking, but you drink a few glasses of wine whenever you need to relax, try meditating or taking a bath instead. You'll still feel more relaxed, but you'll have done it without engaging in unwanted behaviors.

Make Your Negative Habits More Difficult

Remember that habits only happen when they aren't too tricky. If you want to stop engaging in bad habits, try finding a way to make them harder to accomplish. The more difficult the task is to do, the less likely you'll be to do that task.

Discover the Root

Sometimes the reason we engage in bad habits is more complicated than we might initially think. Overeating, for example, often isn't due to you being hungry all the time. You might feel overly hungry when you're tired or stressed, and so, on days when you didn't get enough sleep or are experiencing high levels of anxiety, you might find yourself unconsciously snacking throughout the entire day.

So often, bad habits are created as a type of coping mechanism. Understanding why you've formed that coping mechanism will help you address the root problem, and determine healthier ways to deal with that problem.

Engage in Healthy Routines

A lot of times, building a good habit requires a healthy lifestyle. If you're trying to eat healthy but are constantly engaging in other unhealthy behaviors, it will be a lot harder to make that new habit stick. Making small changes in your daily life that support your new habits will make it easier for you to form those positive behaviors.

Swap Out Your Bad Habits

Sometimes changing a bad habit in one go is too monumental of a task. Smoking is a typical example of this type of habit. It's famously hard to quit smoking all at once. That's why there are things like nicotine patches and gum, as these will, slowly but surely, help you successfully quit smoking.

If you find you have a bad habit that you can't seem to shake, no matter how hard you try, you might need to start smaller. Figure out small ways you can begin to transform that habit, and, in time, you'll be able to swap out that habit entirely.

Create Intrinsic Motivation

Intrinsic motivation comes from within. So often, we're results-oriented. We have our goals, and are motivated to reach them not because of ourselves, but because of the external idea of accomplishing that goal.

Intrinsic motivation, however, is when we are motivated by ourselves. We want to change, so we work to make that change occur solely because it is what we want to do with our lives.

To create intrinsic motivation within your life, you'll need to learn that you are in control of your choices, and that you have the freedom to act how you desire. From there, you can gain personal satisfaction through these choices and actions.

It's a powerful force, the desire to change for your own sake. That internal fire can make all the difference in creating a positive lifestyle that benefits and supports you, as you move forward into the future.

While those seven steps are some of the most powerful ways to eliminate bad habits, there are still many more behaviors and mindsets you can adopt to help your new habits stick.

Things like writing reminders, making a schedule and sticking to it, finding people who will support you, and being kind to yourself are all excellent tips you can use to help your new habits take root in your life.

Remember that not everything will work best for you. Some people thrive when they have a strict routine, while others prefer more flexibility and freedom in their day. If you like your life to be scheduled, having a set time each day when you work on new habits will work for you. If you're the opposite of that kind of person, having those written reminders—so you can practice your new routine whenever you feel it is the right time for you—is a better choice.

It might take a few tries before you make a new, positive habit stick. If that's the case for you, don't worry. Just keep trying new ways until you find the right way for yourself. After all, there isn't a blueprint for forming new habits. It's a personalized process, so what works for someone else won't necessarily fit your life.

The Habit That Can Change Your Life: Gratitude

If I had to pick the single best habit you could incorporate into your life, I would choose gratitude. Practicing gratitude is one of the best things that you can do for yourself, as it can improve your life in so many ways, from your mental well-being to your interpersonal relationships.

Gratitude is about noticing and appreciating the good things in your life. There are similarities between practicing gratitude and the theme of the first chapter, where I encouraged you to take the time to celebrate and recognize all that you had already accomplished.

When we turn our gazes to the future, we forget to appreciate the present. While it isn't a bad thing to be future-focused, it's important to remember to take some of that focus and turn it onto your current situation. If you're too future-oriented, you might become obsessed with the life you could have, and lose sight of why you're reaching for the future in the first place.

As challenging as it can be, life is filled with small victories and pockets of joy. Your train showing up on time, seeing an old friend, or watching a flower bloom are small moments that can be overlooked in the greater scheme of things; simple yet beautiful moments that you should appreciate.

The stance of psychology when it comes to gratitude is a positive one. Psychologists strongly believe that practicing gratitude leads to greater feelings of happiness in life. By spending as little as five minutes a day on gratitude practices, you'll feel happier, healthier, more inclined to positivity, and generally more optimistic about life.

Getting into the habit of gratitude isn't a difficult task, either. Just like all habits, it only requires a little time and effort before having the mindset of gratitude becomes second nature.

How to Practice Gratitude

When you begin to practice gratitude, the first thing you need to do is to observe the world around you. Through these observations, you'll start to see, more and more, all that you have to be thankful for in your life.

Take special note of the times you say "thank you." How many times a day do you say those words? How often is it genuinely felt, and how often is it something of an afterthought, almost like a reflex?

It's astonishing, once you begin to observe life in this way, the number of reflexive thank-yous that intersperse your days. When someone holds the door for you, when you get off a bus and thank the driver, when someone hands you something you asked for, when someone makes room for you to walk by—there are many times in which you might say thank you without even really noticing.

These small moments are worthy of gratitude and thankfulness, as they're the small moments of kindness that make up so much of our daily lives. It's so easy to get caught up in the negative. You turn on the news, and everything looks bleak, and that negativity infects your mind and heart. Remembering and honoring these small moments is a way to beat back some of that negativity and remind yourself that, even if these moments never make it on the news, they're still important and worth celebrating.

Once you're better at observing those moments, pause before saying thank you in an off-handed manner. Consider why you feel gratitude toward another person in this moment, and allow yourself to acknowledge and experience that gratitude in its entirety. Then, and only then, thank the other person.

In doing so, your thanks will come from a place of genuine emotion and caring. That honesty is something other people pick up on, and that sincere thanks could make all the difference in their day. After all, gratitude isn't just about improving your life. It's about using sincere appreciation to improve the lives of others as well.

Ultimately, practicing gratitude comes down to two key elements. The first is acknowledging, appreciating, and affirming the good things that you receive in your life. The second is doing the same for the other people in your life, and acknowledging all the good they provide you.

Incorporating Gratitude Into Your Life

There are so many ways you can incorporate gratitude into your daily life. Depending on your preferences, some ways will suit you better than others. However, I would recommend at least trying gratitude journaling.

Gratitude journaling is perhaps the most well-known gratitude technique. Basically, at the end of each day, you write the things you are thankful for in your journal. If something specific stood out to you, include that in your journal. Make a note of the joys you have experienced, both big and small, and keep them in your journal to remind you of life's beautiful things.

This practice is an excellent way to keep up the habit of gratitude. It exists as a record of all the times you were thankful. Having a tangible record like that is something you can look back on in years to come, as a way to remember the beautiful moments you experienced. That sort of reminder can be hugely beneficial during the times in life when you're feeling low, or are struggling to remember why you're on the path you're taking.

Expressing your gratitude more openly will also help you turn gratitude into a habit. Start with your family and friends; loved ones who you love and appreciate, and tell them how grateful you are for their presence in your life.

Genuinely thank them for the small things they do for you, as well as the bigger things. Expressing your gratitude in this way will strengthen your relationships, bringing positivity into your life and theirs.

Going through the motions of gratitude will also boost appreciation in your life. You've heard the phrase "fake it till you make it" before, right? This is the same idea. Even if you aren't familiar with practicing gratitude, going through the motions—writing thank you notes, smiling, verbalizing your thankfulness—will eventually trigger more and more gratitude within you. In time, you won't just be going through the motions. Instead, you'll be genuinely practicing gratitude.

I think that last point is the case for many positive habits you might want to make in your life. They'll eventually become second nature, as you repeatedly engage in these healthy behaviors. Even if they don't initially feel genuine, they'll become an ingrained part of you, just as real as anything else.

When we give ourselves the room to foster positivity in our lives, we open the door for incredible things. It's about more than just reaching your goals, though that is a definite benefit of engaging in positive habits. It's about taking care of yourself, and treating yourself with the kindness, respect, and grace you deserve. It's about loving yourself and understanding that you deserve to be taken care of—especially by yourself.

Chapter 6

Balance

Take Care of Your Body and Mind

"Our bodies are our gardens—our wills are our gardeners."

—William Shakespeare

S hakespeare is certainly onto something with his metaphor, but let's try another: Our body is like a car. The driver is the mind, which thinks, and decides where to go. However, if the driver doesn't put gasoline in the car, or if they don't change the oil (or periodically check it), or they don't take care of the engine, the wheels, the brakes, and so on, then the car—sooner or later—will not be able to take them wherever they want to go.

Even if the car's in tip-top shape, if the driver is too tired or exhausted, the car will likely still not get too far (or get going at all, for that matter).

So it is for all of us: To reach any goal, we must take care of both our body and our mind. They are, ultimately, all we have available throughout the journey—and they aren't something we can change halfway through.

Learning to take care of yourself can be tricky, especially if you're accustomed to taking care of other people first. When you're accustomed to always putting yourself last, you let a lot of your life slide. It's about more than realizing you gave up on some of your previous ambitions. For some of you, it's about the fact that you forgot to take care of yourself as you took care of everyone else.

The reality is that if you want to have the life of your dreams, you will have to do more than work toward those goals. You're also going to have to ensure that you're in a place where you can make those strides and head toward that future. If you aren't taking care of your physical and mental health, you aren't going to be able to put your best efforts forward.

This isn't to say you have to make drastic changes to your life. I can't sit here and tell you that the secret to success in life is to run a marathon every month, or something like that. Instead, I'm saying that the key to success is making sure you're treating yourself properly.

Think about any time you felt unwell, whether it was because you were having a bad day mentally, or you were sick, or perhaps even injured somehow. Whatever the case, consider how feeling unwell in that way affected you. It was likely harder to do even the simplest of tasks. You might have struggled with things that, on other days, would have taken next to no effort.

When I say you have to take care of yourself, I mean this. If you don't take care of yourself, if you don't prioritize your well-being, then you aren't going to be able to do everything you want. However, if you take care of both your body and mind, you'll be better equipped to achieve all you desire.

As I said, it isn't about making massive changes. Instead, taking care of yourself is about recognizing the areas of your life that you might need to pay more attention to; the areas that you've let slide time and time again.

I'll show you the importance of prioritizing these different areas of your life, in order to show you how you can start to take better care of your mind and body. When you're ready to start chasing your dreams, you'll know your lifestyle won't be holding you back.

Sleep: Your Best Friend

Sleeping is a basic human need, but it's one that an overwhelming number of people struggle with. One in three adults living in the United States reported regularly not getting enough sleep (National Heart, Lung, and Blood Institute, 2022).

This is a real problem. When we don't get enough sleep, we set ourselves up for difficulties. After all, getting a good night's sleep is the best way to start to take care of yourself, as when you sleep, you recharge your body. This is how you replenish your energy to be refreshed and ready for each new day. Sleeping is essential for maintaining good health, not just in the short-term, but throughout your entire life.

When you don't get enough sleep, your mental processes are slowed. You're sluggish, groggy, and you tire easily. You're more likely to overeat, as a lack of sleep is tied to many factors that boost your appetite.

It's more than that, though. When you're tired, you aren't yourself. You're more susceptible to stress, prone to emotional outbursts, and you have difficulty regulating your responses to different situations. When you don't get enough sleep, it's harder to fight back against those negative voices in your head; the ones trying to bring you down, and make you think you can't succeed.

Most adults need between seven and nine hours of sleep each night. I want you to take a moment to consider the last time you hit that sleep goal. If you can't even remember the last time you had enough sleep, then it's high time you started to prioritize sleep in your life.

How to Improve Your Sleep

Of course, it isn't necessarily as simple as all that. Getting enough sleep can be challenging, especially if you've had issues with sleep deficiencies in the past, as it's common for people to grow accustomed to a lack of sleep. Over time, less sleep starts to feel normal, and you might not even realize that you are sleep deficient, as that's the level you're used to living with.

However, even if you have grown used to not getting enough sleep, you can still try some of these positive habits to help you reset your sleep schedule and start getting those seven hours of rest each night.

Establish a Realistic Sleep Schedule

You might think having a bedtime is for children, but it's good for adults as well. If you have a set time when you get into bed, you'll be more likely to fall asleep at a reasonable hour, instead of staying up well into the night. When you're consistent with when you go to sleep at night and when you wake up in the morning, you'll gradually grow used to sleeping at those times. Eventually, you'll find yourself with a regular sleep schedule, and a more improved quality of sleep overall.

After all, our bodies follow something known as circadian rhythms. A circadian rhythm is a 24-hour cycle our bodies naturally follow. Our bodies are instinctually set on this loop, aligned with sunrise and sunset. By embracing this cycle, we stop fighting our bodies' natural impulses, and we can sleep the way our body desires.

Increase Your Daily Exposure to Bright Light

Your circadian rhythm is also affected by your exposure to bright, natural light. This rhythm is what tells us to sleep when it's dark, and wake up when it's light out. As such, when we go outside and receive plenty of bright sunlight, we not only energize ourselves during the day, but also set ourselves up for a good night's rest. Even people with more severe sleep issues like insomnia can benefit from more sunlight.

Studies have been conducted on the relationship between sleep and daytime light exposure. One of these studies found that, for people who had experienced at least a year of insomnia, exposure to bright light during the daytime improved sleep efficiency—the time spent asleep while in bed—from 77.5% to 90% (Campbell et al., 1993).

Reduce Blue Light Exposure

More and more, it seems like blue light is everywhere. We're exposed to an incredible amount of blue light each day, from our computer screens to our phones. However, while blue light makes the colors on our screens pop, it's also a significant factor in what keeps so many of us up at night.

When it gets to be later in the evening, try to reduce your exposure to blue light. You can do this by making sure you spend at least an hour before bed offline, or you can use a blue light filter on your phone or laptop.

Cut Back on Caffeine

While having a morning cup of coffee can help you get going and prepare for the day, having it too late in the day can keep you up all night. After all, caffeine is a natural stimulant. That means it stimulates your nervous system and makes it harder for you to relax naturally, which is precisely what you want to avoid when trying to fall asleep.

Try to keep your coffee intake to the morning, and stick to decaf in the afternoon. If you're getting enough sleep at night, you'll likely find yourself craving that afternoon energy boost.

Optimize Your Sleep Environment

Having a comfortable sleep environment where you feel safe and calm is essential to having a good night's sleep. Do your best to ensure your bedroom is a place in which you can relax, and try to keep the lights low, and the temperature on the cooler side, as it's common for people to have a worse quality of sleep when they're overheated.

Take Time to Relax Before Bed

Most of all, give yourself time to unwind before going to bed. Whether by quietly reading a book, reflecting on your day, or taking a relaxing shower or bath, make sure you're engaging in an activity that will help you feel calm, centered, and ready for rest.

These are just a few ways you can try to improve your sleep. However, if you suffer from a severe sleep issue, it might be worth seeking out professional advice to see if there's something your doctor can do to help you.

Sleep is undeniably one of the most restorative things we can do for our health. Having enough rest is the answer for so many ailments. In the long-term, sleeping well can improve your memory, emotional health, immune system, and so much more. Alongside diet and exercise, sleep is one of the best ways to take care of yourself.

Food Is Fuel

Food is essential for survival. Without food, you cannot live. It's what fuels us and keeps us going, giving us the strength we need to navigate the world. Eating nutritious food is a vital part of taking care of yourself since, if you don't fuel your body and mind, you won't be able to do all you dream of doing.

Eating healthy, well-balanced, and nutritious meals boosts your health. Good nutrition is one of the best ways to maintain a healthy weight. It's all too easy to be caught up in fad diets, but the reality is that even if these diets do make you lose weight quickly—which isn't always a healthy thing—they aren't sustainable. As soon as you stop following the diet, you're likely going to gain back any weight you might have lost.

However, teaching yourself to eat healthy, and maintaining good nutrition in your meals, is a sustainable practice. This practice is easy to continue following since it's a lifestyle and not a fad.

Good nutrition is about more than just weight management. The idea that the food you eat only affects what dress size you wear is one of the most damaging beliefs a person can hold. After all, having good nutrition can also boost your immune system, protect you from chronic disease, and even delay the onset of aging.

Not only that, but good nutrition also affects your mental well-being. Spinach, for example, contains high amounts of iron. There is a strong connection between your iron levels and your mental health and mood, and as such, iron deficiencies can contribute to feelings of depression. When you eat enough iron, you manage those negative feelings and protect yourself against mood disorders.

That's only one example too! Other nutrients found in food that make up part of a balanced diet include omega-3 fatty acids and folic acid, which do a lot of work to support mental health and brain function.

Tips for Healthy Eating

Most of us know what healthy eating entails. It's about eating plenty of fruits and vegetables, having whole grains, and eating less sugar and less fried foods. However, you can take a few tips under advisement to make healthy eating easier to incorporate into your daily routines.

Have Variety in Your Diet

You've probably heard the phrase "variety is the spice of life" before, which is especially true for your food. After all, it isn't healthy to eat only salads, so don't let yourself be limited by any preconceived notions you might have about what constitutes healthy eating.

Try new fruits and veggies, look for healthy carbs, and try different types of protein. Remember, too, that fats aren't necessarily bad for you. There are all kinds of healthy fats that provide health benefits, like olive oil, avocados, and nuts. The more variety in your diet, the broader spread of nutrients you'll be receiving. The more nutrients, the better your body will feel and perform.

Choose Healthy Carbs

While carb diets are often lauded as the answer to all your nutritional needs, the truth is that carbs aren't the enemy. They're your body's primary source of energy, so, without any carbs, you'll be more lethargic.

Try choosing healthy carbs, rather than cutting them out of your diet entirely. This includes going for whole grain over white bread, and eating natural sugars rather than processed ones.

Eat Your Five A Day

Five A Day refers to the number of servings of fruits and veggies you should be trying to eat each day. Fruits and vegetables are a great source of so many nutrients and vitamins, and they do a lot of good for your health, like regulating bodily functions and protecting against long-term diseases.

Fresh, frozen, or even blended into a smoothie, no matter how you eat fruits and vegetables, find a way that works for you. It's not about how you eat your Five A Day, it's just about eating them.

Pay Attention to Portions

You can have the healthiest dinner of all time, but that won't matter if you're over or under eating. It's essential to manage your portions to ensure you're getting the right nutrients, energy, and calories. If you eat too little, you won't be getting enough calories. If you overeat, you'll have too many calories. It's a delicate balancing act that gets easier over time.

Pay attention to your hunger and energy levels throughout the day. If you're feeling hungry again an hour after eating, there's a good chance you didn't eat enough. Pay attention, as well, to how you feel after eating a meal. You should feel full, but not uncomfortably so.

You know your body best, so trust your instinct, and listen to what it's telling you. Depending on your lifestyle, you might need more or less food than other people. The amount of food you need to eat, and the types of food you require are a personal thing, the same as with everything in life. What works for someone else might not work for you.

Eating healthy isn't about achieving a perfect life where you never eat a cookie again. It's about taking care of your body and its specific needs, and understanding that it's okay not to eat healthy all the time, so long as you do so most of the time.

Be Active!

Sleep, food, and exercise are the three main pillars of healthy living. Taking care of these three areas sets you up for an overall healthier lifestyle. Each of these aspects of your life contribute significantly to your mental, emotional, and physical health.

When you engage in regular exercise and activity, you'll experience many health benefits. In terms of your physical health, daily exercise can improve your heart health, reduce the risk of stroke, lower your cholesterol levels and blood pressure, and reduce type-2 diabetes.

Not only that, but engaging in physical activity—while requiring you to use energy—actually makes you more energized. This is because of the endorphins that are released when you exercise.

For your mental health, daily physical activity is known to boost your mood due to those same endorphins, as well as improve your focus, decrease your stress, and help distract yourself from negative thoughts.

It only takes 30 minutes a day to experience these benefits. While that might sound like a lot, especially when you lead a busy life, it isn't that much. If you can't exercise every day, don't worry. So long as you're trying to get those 30 minutes at least three times a week, you're setting yourself up for success.

Managing Stress

The more you start to take care of those three pillars of your health, the more you might notice your stress levels decreasing. When you begin to take care of your body and mind in all of these areas, you'll reap many positive benefits. One of the most positive benefits is stress reduction.

Stress affects us all, and sometimes, it does this in ways we don't even realize. High levels of stress make us feel exhausted and unmotivated, and can lead to issues like sleep deficiency, and the all-too-common stress-eating.

There are physical and mental symptoms of stress, and these symptoms often result in behavioral changes. Next time you feel more stressed out, take a step back from the situation and observe your mental, physical, and emotional state.

You might have a headache, your heart might be racing, or you could even be experiencing chest pain. Mentally, you might be overthinking, falling more easily into negative thought spirals, and completely unable to focus. Keep an eye on how you respond to this distress. You might be angrier than usual, or maybe you feel overwhelming sadness. You might find yourself binging on unhealthy food, and exercising less.

This is why learning to manage stress is essential for taking care of yourself. If you can find ways that help you handle your stress, you'll be able to avoid those adverse effects.

There are all kinds of ways to manage stress in your life. Practicing gratitude can help your stress levels, as can other self-care activities like mindfulness and meditation. Getting enough sleep, eating healthily, and exercising regularly will help you manage stress in your life, but so, too, will things like breathing exercises, drinking tea, talking to a close friend or loved one, or even listening to m usic.

Ultimately, the best way to manage stress in your life is to take care of yourself. The best way to take care of yourself is to recognize that you are worth being taken care of, and start to prioritize your needs. Find the ways to treat yourself with kindness and respect, and remember to be gentle with yourself.

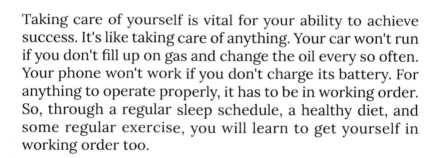

Taking care of yourself is vital for your ability to achieve success. It's like taking care of anything. Your car won't run if you don't fill up on gas and change the oil every so often. Your phone won't work if you don't charge its battery. For anything to operate properly, it has to be in working order. So, through a regular sleep schedule, a healthy diet, and some regular exercise, you will learn to get yourself in working order too.

Chapter 7

Mindset

Choose to Believe in Yourself

*"Each sunrise gives hope to your dreams and
light to your plans."*

—William Ngwako Maphoto

Your mindset is the lens through which you view the world. It's the way you engage with life; the way you think about the reality in which you live. It's the idea of how some people seem to view the world through rose-colored glasses. Everything they experience takes on a rosy sheen because of the way their particular mindset colors their perspective.

Consider the times in your life you went into a situation expecting to have a bad time. Were your expectations proven true? If so, there's a good chance that's because of your frame of mind. You believed you would be unhappy and, by doing so, made yourself miserable.

This is why I've said believing in yourself and remaining optimistic about your journey is essential to your success. There's so much in life that we can't control. Our mindset, however, is something that we do have power over. By choosing to believe in yourself, you are also adopting a mindset where success is not just possible, but inevitable.

How Your Mindset Affects Your Life

It's sometimes hard to see the mindset that you have. It involves reflection and growing your self-awareness, since it is so ingrained in the ways you perceive the world. Your attitude is formed from your experiences, thoughts, desires, and values. If you have been lied to often in the past, for example, there's a good chance you'll begin to develop a mindset of distrusting other people's words.

However, you can change your mindset. By reflecting on your perceptions of the world, examining your actions and reactions, and practicing techniques like mindfulness—wherein you root yourself firmly in the present reality in which you find yourself—you can change your frame of mind.

Types of Mindsets

It's important to remember that we don't have one mindset that constantly propels us through life. The way we think is often determined by the situation in which we find ourselves. This is why it's essential to look at your responses to different scenarios, as you might notice you're more likely to be positive or negative depending on the experience.

Since there is this variation within each person's mindset, there are also several different schools of thought regarding mindsets and how they work to shape our thinking. The first is the idea of a growth mindset versus a fixed mindset.

A growth mindset is based on the idea that we can constantly grow and improve our skills and intelligence. A fixed mindset is the idea that our intelligence and skill levels are fixed. According to this way of thinking, there is only so far each person can go.

A growth mindset encourages accepting what you don't know or can't do, and striving to become better. A fixed mindset fosters an attitude of constantly comparing yourself to others and feeling stagnant in life.

In many ways, there's a connection between the growth versus fixed mindsets, and the optimistic versus pessimistic mindsets. Someone with an optimistic attitude will see the best in other people and situations, and believe in a brighter future. Alternatively, pessimistic people will expect the worst, and look for adverse outcomes.

People with a fixed mindset are likely to be more pessimistic, and more inclined to believe that they can't achieve something. People who have a growth-oriented mind will believe in their ability to reach their dreams and achieve what they set their minds to attain.

Then, there's the risk-taking versus the risk-averse mindsets. These mindsets focus on how willing we are to take risks. If you're generally pessimistic, you'll likely be more risk-averse than an optimistic person, who will see the potential for a positive outcome, and probably take that leap of faith.

When it comes to building the future of your dreams, I encourage you to adopt an optimistic mindset. Be open to the potential of your growth, and the success that that potential will bring about in your life. Allow yourself to take chances, even if you aren't sure of their outcomes. After all, there's no way you can achieve success without taking a few chances. If you avoid all risks, you also avoid all opportunities for change.

Mindset and Your Goals

Having a growth mindset encourages you to embrace learning. If you believe that you can continuously improve, you're more likely to seek opportunities to learn, grow, and change.

Not only that, but a growth mindset helps you learn to manage mistakes and failures. If you have a fixed mindset, failure is an ending, since you believe that if you don't succeed, it's because you were never going to be able to do so
.

However, a growth mindset encourages you to see failure and mistakes as another learning opportunity. They're a way to see how the path you were on might not have been the right one. Through failure, you can discover new ways forward—better ways, in fact—ones that you may never have uncovered, had you not made a mistake in the first place.

By believing in your limitless potential, you free yourself from the constraints of toxic perfectionism, limitations placed on you by yourself and society, and anything else that might be holding you back from success.

Understanding that you can continuously improve upon yourself helps you reduce feelings of burnout, increases motivation, and helps with stress levels. After all, a lot of stress arises from the fear of failure. Accepting that failure is just another opportunity for growth eliminates that avenue for anxiety.

Thoughts are the basis for our actions, whether we're aware of these thoughts or not. When you are careful with your thoughts, you can control your current frame of mind and create the mindset that you would like to have.

When you first start on a task, the direction of your thoughts and, in turn, your mindset can make the difference between achieving a successful outcome or falling short. Think of it this way: You only fail if you accept failure. If you have a growth mindset and refuse to see your failures as failures, and instead view them as further opportunities, you can't fail. You can only grow.

Positive versus Negative Thoughts

The problem many of us face when trying to adopt an optimistic mindset is navigating our negative thoughts. Negative thinking feeds into pessimism, feelings of despair, defeatism, and a generalized sense of stress and worthlessness.

Having a negative attitude can take a real toll on your physical and mental health. It drains you of energy, leaving you feeling wrung out and lifeless. You start to question the validity of these feelings, and if left unchecked, you begin to believe they're true.

This negative thinking, and the downward spiral of your mood, are the first main effect that negative thoughts have on your attitude and perspective on life. Negative thought patterns lead to low moods, with emotions like sadness, hopelessness, fear, and anger coming to the forefront.

Being constantly inundated with these negative emotions, your behavior will also start to fall into those patterns. You'll be more guarded toward others, less likely to take chances, and unwilling to believe in the possibility of change. Your negative thoughts will convince you not to try things because you won't believe in their potential.

This leads to the second significant effect negative thinking has: It halts your progress in life, preventing you from achieving goals. When you're setting goals and starting this journey, you want to feel motivated and excited by the prospect of the future.

Negative thinking, however, holds you back. You begin to pick apart your plans, focusing only on the negative potential, rather than the positive. Eventually, you'll have spent so much time convincing yourself that it isn't worth trying, that you'll give up before starting.

This is how negative thoughts hold you back. You listen to that critical voice in your head which tells you that you can't achieve your goals, and you agree with what it says. This is why, to reach your dreams, you have to learn to recognize, halt, and eliminate those downward thought spirals, and work to embrace a mindset of positivity and hope instead.

Managing Negative Thoughts

Sometimes negative thoughts can seem like the smallest splinter. Even when you pull it out, part of it might break off and stay trapped under the skin, digging in deeper and deeper, and bringing you more and more pain.

It's tricky to learn to stop negative thoughts. For a lot of us, they're almost a habit. To overcome negative thought patterns, to entirely remove that splinter, you first have to learn to recognize negative thoughts.

To begin recognizing when your self-talk is negative, you will have to build up an awareness of your thoughts as they happen. Pay attention to your moods and reactions, then trace your behaviors back to the idea that prompted them. This might be challenging at first, but, over time, it will become easier and easier until you reach a point where you can recognize your thoughts the moment you think them.

Once you've reached that point, you can start to identify your negative self-talk. You should try to watch out for several types of this talk. I've put together a list of some of the more common ones:

Catastrophizing

Have you ever been in line at the airport and found yourself unable to stop worrying about the plane crashing? This type of thinking, wherein you assume the worst-case scenario will happen before you even start doing anything, is known as catastrophizing.

Filtering

Let's say you've presented a proposal at work to ten other people. Nine of those people tell you that they love the idea, while one says they aren't interested. Filtering is when you begin to obsess over that one person's negative response, allowing it to consume your mind until you believe that your proposal wasn't any good, and in doing so, you completely filter out and forget all of the positive feedback you received. It's when you focus solely on the negative, to the complete exclusion of the positive.

Magnifying

Magnifying is like the common phrase "making a mountain out of a molehill." It's the tendency to turn a minor inconvenience into a major problem, obsessing over it until it's all you can think about.

Personalizing

Have you ever had plans with a group of friends, and then had everyone else cancel one by one? Did you then convince yourself that the reason the plans fell apart wasn't that the other people had other things going on in their lives, but instead, it was because everyone hated you? Personalizing is when you see everything as being your fault. Whenever a problem arises, you take all the blame, convincing yourself that the real problem is you.

Polarizing

Polarizing is the tendency many people have to see a situation as being only good or bad. It's like considering a partial success a complete failure. When you engage in polarizing thoughts, you leave no room for nuance or a middle ground. Instead, everything is either positive or negative, with no space in between.

These are only a few examples of negative self-talk, but it's easy to see how common these thinking patterns are, even from these few. I've thought like that before, and I'm sure you have as well.

Once you recognize negative self-talk, the next step is to see how you can change the way you think. One of the best ways to do this is by challenging those negative thoughts.

Challenging Negative Thoughts

Challenging negative self-talk is a significant component of various therapy practices and techniques. Cognitive-behavioral therapy, for example, is entirely centered around the idea of learning how to challenge these negative thoughts, and shifting them in a more positive direction.

When you first recognize a negative thought, question that thought. Ask yourself why you're thinking this way, and challenge the assumption you have unconsciously made. If you can, try to reframe the thought in a more positive way. It's like the idea of creating a positive mantra out of a self-defeating belief. By reframing your thinking, you can turn something negative into something positive.

It doesn't even need to be a massive reversal of your thought process. Sometimes, by simply shifting your perspective, you can completely change how you react to a situation. Take having to use a new computer program at your job to complete a project, for example. Rather than thinking that this won't go well because you've never done it before, try to tell yourself that, since you've never done this before, it's a chance to learn a new skill.

The core basis of the thought—the understanding that you have never done the thing before—hasn't changed. Instead, it's your reaction to this situation that has shifted.

Acknowledging your negative feelings and thoughts is another way to learn to manage them. A lot of us tend to shut down any negative or unpleasant emotion, in order to try and get over that feeling. However, doing this doesn't help us at all. Instead, you have to genuinely feel the emotion to move on from feeling this way.

Sometimes, you have to acknowledge it when you have a negative thought. Allow that thought to exist, recognize it was there, and then let it go. Don't linger on it, don't keep coming back to it; just release it into the world and move on. Some feelings need to be felt, and some thoughts need to be thought.

When you're challenging your negative thoughts, there are several questions you can ask yourself. I've put together a worksheet you can use to help you address and reassess any negative self-talk you may experience. As for the others you can download it by following the link at the end, or if you prefer to do it yourself, here are the steps I suggest:

- Write down your negative thought

- Is there evidence proving this thought?

- If there is evidence, is it past or current evidence?

- Is there evidence disproving this thought?

- How would a friend view this situation?

- Rewrite your thought in a positive light.

- How is it different?

A lot of the time, when you challenge your negative thoughts, they start to fall apart. The evidence you come up with to support your negative thinking is usually rooted in past mistakes, feelings of insecurity, or other various reasons that aren't exactly credible.

Not only that, but when you take the time to write the evidence that contradicts your negative self-talk, that will often be rooted in reality. When you step back from the situation, you can see things more clearly. You'll see that the negative thoughts clouding your mind are nothing more than fleeting moments, and that they aren't true.

Practicing Positive Self-Talk

Another way to combat negative self-talk is to embrace and practice its opposite. Positive self-talk is essential to having an optimistic and growth mindset. It isn't about ignoring all of the troubles and challenges in your path, blithely continuing wearing rose-colored glasses, and ignoring reality. Instead, positive thinking is about understanding and recognizing your power.

Positive self-talk is rooted in the belief in self. It's about trusting in your abilities, and knowing that you are capable of achieving your goals. Focus on your life and objectives, and ignore what others are doing with their lives. When you believe in yourself, the accomplishments of others aren't a source of envy. So, don't compare your successes to those of other people. Instead, take joy in their victories, as well as your own.

One tip I have is to pay attention to your language, especially after setbacks. If you think, "I should have done this," you aren't treating your setback as a learning opportunity. Instead, you're taking this stumble as an opportunity to beat yourself up. Rather than focusing on what you should have done, focus on what you will do next t ime.

Don't force positivity, either. Some days you're going to feel a little down, and that's okay. Like I said, sometimes negative emotions need to be experienced, so allow yourself to do so. Just remember that they aren't the only emotions you have. Happiness and joy still exist, even when you're subsumed in sadness.

The best thing you can do to help yourself foster a mindset of optimism is to surround yourself with positivity. Fill your days with things that bring you joy. Surround yourself with people who also practice positivity, rather than those who constantly complain and bring you down. When you make room for positivity in your life, incredible things will follow.

Chapter 8

Celebrate

Each Milestone Helps
You Grow

*"My will shall shape the future. Whether I fail
or succeed shall be no one's doing but my own.
I am the force. I can clear any obstacle before
me or I can be lost in the maze. My choice. My
responsibility. Win or lose; only I hold the key to
my destiny."*

—Elaine Maxwell

T he road ahead of you might seem long, as it stretches
into the unknown future. You might not know how
far it will lead you, but you're determined to walk its
length until the end of the road. It can be hard to keep
up your determination with such a journey. That's why
it's so important to remember to pay attention to every
checkpoint, every milestone, and to celebrate each victory,
big and small, that you reach along the way.

Celebrating your milestones is the best way to keep yourself motivated. It's a way of taking a moment to take pride in what you have accomplished, and a way to observe your personal growth.

When you're caught up in the mindset of constantly achieving more and more; of heading toward a specific future, you risk blinding yourself to the progress you've made. You might not see how far you have come, how much you have already done, and how much you've changed during the journey. Honoring these milestones, however, reminds you of these accomplishments, and why you're doing what you're doing.

These small moments of celebration encourage you to keep moving forward, as with each small victory you mark, you'll be more enthusiastic and excited to achieve the next. By recognizing your current progress, you ready yourself for future improvement. After all, each step forward, and each milestone reached, is another step forward on your journey. It's a sign of your constant progress; of your unrelenting quest toward your dreams.

Celebrating your progress is also a form of reflection. When you commemorate your achievements, you are not only motivating yourself to continue, but you're also honoring your growth as a person. It's a way of looking back at your former self and being grateful for all the hard work you did to transform into your present self.

Looking back at the distance you've traveled reminds you of the importance of the journey you're on, that the steps you take to reach your dreams are as meaningful as the dreams themselves.

Ways to Celebrate

Honoring your accomplishments fosters pride within you. Pride is something that has a lot of negative connotations. It's conflated with arrogance, and is even counted among the seven deadly sins.

However, the reality is that pride isn't something to be scorned. Taking pride in your success is a good thing. Pride can be incredibly empowering, and it's also one of a select few emotions that creates success.

Things like pride and gratitude are, in many ways, the backbone of motivation. When you're grateful for the good things in your life and you take pride in your accomplishments, you create within yourself a growing source of inner strength, one that can fuel your willpower and drive.

Celebrating versus Rewarding

Remembering to take pride in your accomplishments while continuing to practice gratitude is the key to making sure you're celebrating your milestones in a healthy way. As your pride helps you stay motivated and reach for the future, your gratitude reminds you of where you have been, and what you have already achieved.

After all, a celebration isn't the same as a reward. You reward yourself when something is over. It's the end prize—the sign that you have completed your journey, and that there is no further leg to maneuver. On the other hand, celebrating your success is about appreciating the progress you've made, and becoming motivated for where you still have to reach.

The difference between celebration and reward is, in many ways, reflective of the difference between intrinsic and extrinsic motivation. As I mentioned in Chapter 5, intrinsic motivation is about internal motivation. The drive within you propels you forward, changing and reaching your goals because it's what you desire. This type of motivation is focused on the journey, rather than the outcome.

Extrinsic motivation is the opposite. When you're motivated by what you might reach, an external factor propels you forward. While this isn't a bad thing, especially when you're first starting, extrinsic motivation will run out faster than intrinsic.

When we reward our successes, we set a precedent for motivating ourselves through external means. Celebrating our milestones, however, fosters intrinsic motivation, where we are motivated by our sense of pride and gratitude.

Healthy Ways to Celebrate

There are considerations to take into account when celebrating your success. Going on a wild binge of some sort isn't healthy, and neither is doing something like celebrating your progress by backsliding into old behaviors. A celebration doesn't have to be wild or over the top. Often it's the smaller, more personal celebrations that are more meaningful and beneficial.

One healthy way to celebrate is to take some time for yourself. Have a day off where you do something you enjoy. This might include engaging in a fun hobby, or taking a day trip somewhere nice. Treating yourself to a massage is another example of how to celebrate by taking the time to treat yourself with care.

Including others in your celebration is also a great way to honor your accomplishments. Having those who have supported you in your journey take part in your victories will remind you of all the love you have in your life, and it will also make those loved ones feel valued in return.

This is a great way to strengthen bonds and build deeper relationships. Going out for dinner, or having your friends over for a game night, are great ways to include them in your celebrations.

Reflection, as well, is a healthy way to celebrate your milestones. When you reflect on your success, you can see what you did to help you achieve this accomplishment. Then, armed with that knowledge and awareness, you can replicate those actions to help you reach further milestones.

―――――◆O◆―――――

The Importance of Reflection

Reflection is not just a crucial part of celebrating your milestones, but also of understanding them. When you reflect on your achievements, you take the time to understand the journey you took to reach this place, how you did so, and what steps you took which worked for you.

Doing this builds awareness of your skills, both those you previously held, and any new ones you gained. By understanding your skillset, you'll be able to see ways to replicate your success, and new paths you can take to achieve further accomplishments.

More than that, though, reflection is about building self-awareness. When you look back on your journey, you look back on yourself. You see who you were, and compare that to who you have become. It's a way of better understanding how this journey has shaped you, and it can help you recognize those smaller moments of personal growth that are easily overlooked.

You might gain a new perspective on yourself and your past when you reflect on your journey. It can make sense of things that seemed previously incomprehensible, and can show you different parts of yourself you might not have known existed.

Reflection also helps you continue with your plans to achieve your goals. When you reflect, you look at what went right and wrong. You'll be more equipped to handle future setbacks, since you have had experience navigating previous mistakes. You'll also have a better idea of the areas you need to focus and improve on, in order to be more effective in reaching the next milestone.

Self-reflection also boosts self-esteem. By looking at your victories and allowing yourself to feel pride, you prove your capabilities. You aren't "faking it until you make it" anymore. Instead, you're entirely aware of what you can accomplish, and you gain a sense of confidence born from that understanding.

The Gibbs' Reflective Cycle

When you reflect on your successes, you are, in many ways, learning by looking at what you have done. You look back on your experience, and take lessons from that time to use in the future. In many ways, this ability to learn from experience is the true power of reflection.

In 1988, Professor Graham Gibbs, an American sociologist, published *Learning by Doing: A Guide to Teaching Methods*. In this book, he proposed a cycle known as the Gibbs' Reflective Cycle to help people reflect on their experiences in more detail. This way, they can gain the most insight from their reflection, and be better equipped for their next steps.

This cycle includes six phases. These phases are description, feelings, evaluation, analysis, conclusion, and action plan.

- The first phase is the **description** of the experience. During this phase, you describe what happened in detail. This should only include the stark facts of what happened, and not any personal opinions on the situation.

- The second phase is your **feelings** and thoughts regarding the experience. This is when you would reflect on the way you felt during this time, and how you think and feel about the situation in the present moment.

- Next is the **evaluation** of the experience. When evaluating what happened, remember both the good and bad. Take the time to reflect on what worked, what didn't work, and what you contributed to the experience. Do your best to be as objective as possible during this phase.

- **Analyzing** the experience is the fourth phase. This is the moment where you take the details of the experience and analyze them, so you can extract meaning from the events. You might want to ask yourself "why" questions. During the evaluation phase, you might ask, "what went wrong?" while during this phase, you would ask, "why did that go wrong?"

- The fifth phase is the **conclusion** of the experience. This is when you look at your details, feelings, and analysis, and determine what happened and why. You conclude what you have learned from this experience, and can begin to see how you could act differently in the future.

- Finally, there's the sixth phase. In this phase, you create an **action plan** for what you would do differently next time. Based on your conclusions, you can create a plan for different solutions. Be sure to consider different approaches you could have taken, and how they might have affected the situation differently, as this will help you determine the right path to take next time.

I encourage you to use this cycle to help guide you during your journey. Reflecting on your accomplishments will help you reach your fullest potential. After all, this can be helpful even after you've achieved your goals. Life is a continuous cycle of learning and self-improvement. You only stop growing when you stop trying to change.

Through reflection and celebration, your successes along the way will feel more meaningful. You'll better understand your purpose, as your little victories will bring more and more happiness into your life.

Conclusion

I want you, now, to take a moment to reflect on your dreams, past and present. Consider what they mean to you, and how they make you feel, deep in your heart. Now, think about how your life would look if you made them into a reality. It brings a smile to your face, doesn't it?

When I started setting goals and planning my new future, it felt like I was doing something crazy. Just the idea of starting those first steps was overwhelming. However, the trip was more than worthwhile. There has never been a single moment that I regretted on my journey, and I am so thrilled that you are taking those first steps too.

Take everything I learned, and use it to make your way forward smoother. Remember to get your affairs in order, both mentally and financially, before beginning. Look inward and discover your true values and desires and, from what you find out, create a dream that fills you with hope.

When you set your goals, remember the importance of creating SMART goals. Create plans to achieve lifetime dreams that are peppered with smaller goals to act as milestones along the way. Work to maintain good, positive habits, along with an optimistic mindset, and never forget to take the time to celebrate your accomplishments and reflect on everything you have achieved and learned along this incredible journey.

Most of all, though, remember that you deserve this. You deserve to chase your dreams. You deserve to live a life filled with your passions. When you wake up in the morning, you should be excited about what the day holds.

It's never too early or too late to plan for your future. You only have one life, and it isn't over yet. So, find a way to live a life that brings you joy, and spend your days smiling. You can always keep growing, changing, achieving new things, and reaching new heights. Your dreams are—and have always been—within your grasp.

Maybe your life didn't go the way you thought it would when you were a kid. Perhaps you gave up on old dreams to make room for new ones. The dreams you once held so dear might not ring true for you any longer.

Whatever the case, know that what you want now, at this moment, matters. If you love something, you should do what you can to have it in your life. Don't worry about what other people have done. Don't worry about what other people will say or think. Focus on yourself for once, and pursue a future that you desire.

There were so many things that brought me overwhelming joy in the life I had before I decided to chase my dreams. It was a good life, and I fondly look back on it. However, happiness isn't finite. If you feel there is something out there that can bring even more joy to you, then it's worth trying.

Julia Child, for example, didn't start cooking until she was 40 years old. When she was nearly 50, she worked on her famous book *Mastering the Art of French Cooking*. Even later in life, she found a passion, and worked to build that passion into her life.

Vera Wang, the fashion designer, didn't start her career path until she was in her 40s. Before that, she pursued other dreams, such as figure skating and journalism. For her, what she wanted at one point wasn't what she wanted forever. However, she didn't give up—she kept pursuing her different passions, making all kinds of dreams come true.

Just as these women have pursued their passions, so too can you. Taking everything I've learned and imparted upon you, I know that you are fully equipped to take your first steps on this incredible journey toward planning a future that sets you free. You have all the tools you need! All that's left is for you to take all your strength, determination, and motivation, and begin.

References

- AAUW. (2020). *The STEM gap: Women and girls in science, technology, engineering and math.* AAUW: Empowering Women since 1881. https://www.aauw.org/resources/research/the-stem-gap/

- Active Health. (2021). *What is good nutrition and why is it important?* Active Health. https://www.activehealth.sg/read/nutrition/what-is-good-nutrition-and-why-is-it-important

- Agarwal, P. (2018, December 17). *Here is how unconscious bias holds women back.* Forbes. https://www.forbes.com/sites/pragyaagarwaleurope/2018/12/17/here-is-how-unconscious-bias-holds-women-back/?sh=14ec052c2d4f

- Alexander, R. (2019, October). *How to start a savings plan.* Monzo. https://monzo.com/blog/2019/10/15/savings-plan

- Alford, C. (2022, February 17). *11 reasons why it's important to follow your dreams.* Lifehack.

https://www.lifehack.org/articles/communicatio
n/11-reasons-why-its-important-follow-your-dre
ams.html

- Asana Team. (2021, October 22). *The Eisenhower Matrix: How to prioritize your to-do list.* Asana. https://asana.com/resources/eisenhower-matrix

- Ayn Rand Quotes. (n.d.). BrainyQuote.com. Retrieved April 21, 2022, from BrainyQuote.com: https://www.brainyquote.com/quotes/ayn_rand_124992

- Babauta, L. (2018, November 16). *22 secrets to discovering your dream and living it.* Dumb Little Man. https://www.dumblittleman.com/22-secrets-to-discovering-your-dream/

- Battles, M. (2016, December 19). *15 ways to practice positive self-talk for success.* Lifehack. https://www.lifehack.org/504756/self-talk-determines-your-success-15-tips

- Better Health Channel. (2018). *Physical activity - it's important.* Vic.gov.au. https://www.betterhealth.vic.gov.au/health/healthyliving/physical-activity-its-important

- Bleidorn, W., Arslan, R. C., Jaap J. A. Denissen, Rentfrow, P. J., Gebauer, J. E., Potter, J., & Gosling, S. D. (2016). Age and gender differences in self-esteem—A cross-cultural window. *Journal of Personality and Social Psychology, 111*(3), 396–410. https://doi.org/10.1037/pspp0000078

- Boddy-Evans, M. (2018, March 4). *What is negative*

space in art? LiveAbout.
https://www.liveabout.com/negative-space-defin
ition-2573838

- Bonfire Yoga. (2015, August 5). *5 steps to discover
your life's ambition.* Bonfire.
https://www.bonfireyoga.com.au/events-and-blo
gs/blog/5-steps-to-discover-your-lifes-ambition
/

- Bostock, J. (2014). *The meaning of success: Insights
from women at cambridge.* Cambridge University
Press.

- Campbell, S. S., Dawson, D., & Anderson, M. W.
(1993). Alleviation of sleep maintenance insomnia
with timed exposure to bright light. *Journal of the
American Geriatrics Society, 41*(8), 829–836.
https://doi.org/10.1111/j.1532-5415.1993.tb06179.x

- Carvalho, I. (2021, January 14). *How to time blocking
your day with Eisenhower Matrix.* Medium.
https://igor-a-carvalho.medium.com/how-to-tim
e-blocking-your-day-with-eisenhower-matrix-a17
8de8eda19

- Chowdhury, M. R. (2022, February 15). *The science &
psychology of goal-setting* 101. PositivePsychology.
https://positivepsychology.com/goal-setting-psy
chology/

- Clarke, J. (2021, October 7). *Healthy ways to celebrate
success.* Verywell Mind.
https://www.verywellmind.com/healthy-ways-to
-celebrate-success-4163887

- Collins, B. (2020, March 3). *The Pomodoro technique*

explained. Forbes. https://www.forbes.com/sites/bryancollinseurop e/2020/03/03/the-pomodoro-technique/?sh=cf f664739857

• Crespo, R. (2019, October 16). *37 examples of personal goals you can start setting today*. Minimalism Made Simple. https://www.minimalismmadesimple.com/home/ personal-goals/

• Crowell, A. (2019, December 6). *3 ways brainstorming can help you plan out your future*. Everyday Power. https://everydaypower.com/brainstorming-exerc ises-for-your-future/

• DeSteno, D. (2016, August 22). *The connection between pride and persistence*. Harvard Business Review. https://hbr.org/2016/08/the-connection-betwee n-pride-and-persistence

• Eatough, E. (2021, December 7). *Building good habits in your life (and ditching bad ones)*. Better Up. https://www.betterup.com/blog/building-habits

• Elaine Maxwell Quotes. (n.d.). Good Reads. Retrieved April 21, 2022, from GoodReads.com: https://www.goodreads.com/quotes/717566-my- will-shall-shape-the-future-whether-i-fail-or

• Elmer, J. (2020, July 1). *5 ways to stop spiraling negative thoughts from taking control*. Healthline. https://www.healthline.com/health/mental-healt h/stop-automatic-negative-thoughts

- Evans, L., & Hardy, L. (2002). Injury rehabilitation: A goal-setting intervention study. *Research Quarterly for Exercise and Sport, 73*(3), 310–319. https://doi.org/10.1080/02701367.2002.10609025

- Financial Wolves. (2021, January 10). *9 reasons why personal finance is important*. Financial Wolves. https://financialwolves.com/why-is-personal-finance-important/

- Frothingham, S. (2019, October 24). *How Long Does It Take for a New Behavior to Become automatic?* Healthline. https://www.healthline.com/health/how-long-does-it-take-to-form-a-habit

- Gourani, S. (2019, July 29). *Why most women give up on their dreams*. Forbes. https://www.forbes.com/sites/soulaimagourani/2019/07/29/why-most-women-give-up-on-their-dreams/?sh=58e0f7172082

- Guina, R. (2019, May 1). *How to organize your finances with a financial inventory*. Cash Money Life. https://cashmoneylife.com/financial-inventory/

- Guise, S. (2013). *Mini habits: Smaller habits, bigger results*. CreateSpace Independent Publishing Platform.

- Head, A. (2021, December 31). *Overwhelmed by new year's resolutions? A life coach on 11 ways to make them a reality*. Marie Claire. https://www.marieclaire.co.uk/life/health-fitness/goals-for-2022-724520

- Ho, L. (2022, February 4). *20 personal SMART goals examples to improve your life*. Lifehack. https://www.lifehack.org/864427/examples-of-personal-smart-goals

- HSPH Staff. (2013, November 6). *Plate power – 10 tips for healthy eating*. The Nutrition Source; Harvard T.H. Chan School of Public Health. https://www.hsph.harvard.edu/nutritionsource/2013/11/06/healthy-eating-ten-nutrition-tips-for-eating-right/

- Hunt, A. (2018, November 5). *How to find motivation to chase your dreams when life is overwhelming*. The Life Hunt. https://thelifehunt.com/how-to-find-motivation-to-chase-your-dreams-when-life-is-overwhelming/

- Indeed Editorial Team. (2021, February 22). *15 tips for goal setting*. Indeed Career Guide. https://www.indeed.com/career-advice/career-development/goal-setting-tips

- Jespersen, C. (2022, April 4). *How to save money: 22 proven ways*. NerdWallet. https://www.nerdwallet.com/article/finance/how-to-save-money

- Kagan, J. (2020, October 5). *Microsavings*. Investopedia. https://www.investopedia.com/terms/m/microsavings.asp

- Kendrick, T. (2016, March 21). *7 tips for planning your day*. Tonia Kendrick.

https://toniakendrick.com/how-to-plan-your-da
y/

- Kenton, W. (2022, February 9). *Personal finance.*
  Investopedia.
  https://www.investopedia.com/terms/p/persona
  lfinance.asp

- Lally, P., van Jaarsveld, C. H. M., Potts, H. W. W., &
  Wardle, J. (2009). How are habits formed: Modelling
  habit formation in the real world. *European Journal
  of Social Psychology, 40*(6), 998–1009.
  https://doi.org/10.1002/ejsp.674

- Lee, H.-S., Chao, H.-H., Huang, W.-T., Chen,
  S. C.-C., & Yang, H.-Y. (2020). Psychiatric
  disorders risk in patients with iron deficiency
  anemia and association with iron supplementation
  medications: A nationwide database analysis. BMC
  Psychiatry, 20(1).
  https://doi.org/10.1186/s12888-020-02621-0

- Long, B. (n.d.). *How to take A fearless financial
  inventory (the easy way).* Zero Debt Coach.
  Retrieved April 11, 2022, from
  https://www.zerodebtcoach.com/blog/how-to-t
  ake-a-fearless-financial-inventory

- Lowinger, J. (2021, August 16). *How your mindset
  affects outcomes.* Mind Strength.
  https://drjodie.com.au/blog/how-your-mindset-
  affects-outcomes

- M, D. (2016, September 24). *15 reasons women give
  up their dreams.* TheTalko.
  https://www.thetalko.com/15-reasons-women-gi
  ve-up-their-dreams/

- Martins, J. (2021, March 22). *7 tips to start time blocking today*. Asana. https://asana.com/resources/what-is-time-block ing

- Maryville University. (2021, November 17). *The importance of celebrating milestones*. Maryville Online. https://online.maryville.edu/blog/importance-of -celebrating-milestones/

- Mawer, R. (2020, February 28). *17 proven tips to sleep better at night*. Healthline. https://www.healthline.com/nutrition/17-tips-to -sleep-better

- Maya Angelou Quotes. (n.d.). Good Reads. Retrieved April 21, 2022, from GoodReads.com: https://www.goodreads.com/quotes/7273813-do- the-best-you-can-until-you-know-better-then

- Mayo Clinic. (2021, March 24). *Stress symptoms: Effects on your body and behavior*. Mayo Clinic. https://www.mayoclinic.org/healthy-lifestyle/str ess-management/in-depth/stress-symptoms/art -20050987

- Mayo Clinic Staff. (2017). *Positive thinking: Stop negative self-talk to reduce stress*. Mayo Clinic. https://www.mayoclinic.org/healthy-lifestyle/str ess-management/in-depth/positive-thinking/art -20043950

- McMullen, L. (2020, February 6). *3 main budget categories*. NerdWallet. https://www.nerdwallet.com/article/finance/bu dget-categories

- Melissa. (n.d.). *Celebrating success*. Skills You Need. https://www.skillsyouneed.com/ps/celebrating-s uccess.html

- Mindful Staff. (2021, November 16). *How to practice gratitude*. Mindful. https://www.mindful.org/how-to-practice-gratit ude/

- MindTools Content Team. (n.d.). *The power of good habits: Using high-performance habits to achieve significant goals*. MindTools. https://www.mindtools.com/pages/article/powe r-good-habits.htm

- MindTools Content Team. (2009). *Personal goal setting: Planning to live your life your way*. MindTools. https://www.mindtools.com/page6.html

- MindTools Content Team. (2016, March 9). SMART *goals: How to make your goals achievable*. Mindtools. https://www.mindtools.com/pages/article/smart -goals.htm

- MindTools Content Team. (2019). *Gibbs' reflective cycle: Helping people learn from experience*. MindTools. https://www.mindtools.com/pages/article/reflec tive-cycle.htm

- Modern Brown Girl. (2020, August 12). *7 famous women who achieved success on their own time*. Her Agenda. https://heragenda.com/p/7-famous-women-who -achieved-success-on-their-own-time/

- National Heart, Lung, and Blood Institute. (2013, February 13). *Tips for getting active.* NIH. https://www.nhlbi.nih.gov/health/educational/wecan/get-active/getting-active.htm

- National Heart, Lung, and Blood Institute. (2022, March 24). *Sleep deprivation and deficiency: What are sleep deprivation and deficiency?* NIH. https://www.nhlbi.nih.gov/health/sleep-deprivation

- Neidel, C. (2021, January 21). *Free Budget Spreadsheets and budget templates.* NerdWallet. https://www.nerdwallet.com/article/finance/free-budget-spreadsheets-templates

- Ong, J. (2021, August 17). *10 benefits of self-reflection: Experience plus scientific papers.* Ongjason.com. https://ongjason.com/what-are-the-benefits-of-self-reflection/

- Pacheco, D. (2022, March 11). *Why do we need sleep?* Sleep Foundation. https://www.sleepfoundation.org/how-sleep-works/why-do-we-need-sleep

- Psychology Today Staff. (2019). *Gratitude.* Psychology Today. https://www.psychologytoday.com/ca/basics/gratitude

- Ralph Waldo Emerson Quotes. (n.d.) Quote Fancy. Retrieved April 21, 2022, from QuoteFancy.com: https://quotefancy.com/quote/608/Ralph-Waldo-Emerson-Do-not-go-where-the-path-may-lead-go-instead-where-there-is-no-path

- Reale, A. (n.d.). *3 steps to create your own mantra.* Lumitory. Retrieved April 12, 2022, from https://lumitory.com/blogs/lumitory-blog/3-ste ps-to-create-your-own-personal-mantra

- Reese, N. (2019, July 3). *10 simple ways to relieve stress.* Healthline. https://www.healthline.com/health/10-ways-to-relieve-stress

- Riopel, L. (2022, March 24). *The importance, benefits, and value of goal setting.* PositivePsychology. https://positivepsychology.com/benefits-goal-set ting/

- Sarah Ban Breathnach Quotes. (n.d.). BrainyQuote.com. Retrieved April 21, 2022, from BrainyQuote.com: https://www.brainyquote.com/quotes/sarah_ban _breathnach_108282

- Scott, S. (2020, August 1). *31 benefits of gratitude: The ultimate science-backed guide.* Happier Human. https://www.happierhuman.com/benefits-of-grat itude/

- Scroggs, L. (n.d.-a). *The complete guide to time blocking.* Todoist. https://todoist.com/productivity-methods/time-blocking

- Scroggs, L. (n.d.). *The Pomodoro technique – why it works & how to do it.* Todoist. https://todoist.com/productivity-methods/pomo doro-technique

- Shortsleeve, C. (2018, August 28). 5

science-approved ways to break a bad habit. Time. https://time.com/5373528/break-bad-habit-scie nce/

- Silber, D. (2021, September 14). *The real effects of negative thinking.* LinkedIn. https://www.linkedin.com/pulse/real-effects-ne gative-thinking-dr-debi-silber

- Silver, C. (2022, February 3). *The ultimate guide to financial literacy.* Investopedia. https://www.investopedia.com/guide-to-financial -literacy-4800530

- Smith, J. (2020, September 25). *Growth vs fixed mindset: How what you think affects what you achieve.* Mindset Health. https://www.mindsethealth.com/matter/growth- vs-fixed-mindset

- The Peak Performance Center. (2020). *Benefits of goal setting.* Thepeakperformancecenter.com. https://thepeakperformancecenter.com/develop ment-series/skill-builder/personal-effectiveness /goal-setting/benefits-of-goal-setting/

- The University of Edinburgh. (2020, November 11). *Gibbs' reflective cycle.* The University of Edinburgh. https://www.ed.ac.uk/reflection/reflectors-toolk it/reflecting-on-experience/gibbs-reflective-cycl e

- Tracy, B. (2019, March 4). *How and why to create A SMART goals template.* Brian Tracy's Self Improvement & Professional Development Blog. https://www.briantracy.com/blog/personal-succ ess/smart-goals/

- USDA My Plate. (2020). *Healthy eating for adults*. Myplate.gov. https://www.myplate.gov/tip-sheet/healthy-eating-adults

- Walker, A. (2020, February 20). Why do so many women have such a complex relationship with food? Stylist. https://www.stylist.co.uk/life/recipes/why-do-so-many-women-have-a-complex-relationship-with-food/232018

- William Ngwako Maphoto Quotes. (n.d.). Some Lines for You. Retrieved April 21, 2022, from SomeLinesForYou.com: https://www.somelinesforyou.com/quote/image/36288

- William Shakespeare Quotes. (n.d.). AllAuthor.com. Retrieved April 21, 2022, from AllAuthor.com: https://allauthor.com/quote/154088/

- Wood, W., & Neal, D. T. (2007). A new look at habits and the habit-goal interface. *Psychological Review*, 114(4), 843–863. https://doi.org/10.1037/0033-295x.114.4.843

- Young, S. H. (2021, December 16). *18 tricks to make new habits stick*. Lifehack. https://www.lifehack.org/articles/featured/18-tricks-to-make-new-habits-stick.html

- Zig Ziglar Quotes. (n.d.). BrainyQuote.com. Retrieved April 21, 2022, from BrainyQuote.com: https://www.brainyquote.com/quotes/zig_ziglar_380875

About Author

Lara Spadetto is an Italian author and figurative artist who loves to travel, cook and experiment with her painting. She is an avid reader and when she is not immersed in the creation of her canvases, she devotes herself to writing. She loves to relax by taking long walks in nature.

After living in Italy, Spain, and the UAE, she now lives permanently in the UK with her 3 children and her beloved dog Maia.

Lara wants to inspire and motivate those who need to rediscover the strength they already have, but whose existence they have forgotten. She wants to encourage them to rekindle the vital spark that time, and false beliefs, have faded.

You can visit her website at: laraspadetto.com

To download the suggested worksheets go to: laraspadetto.com/planyourfuture-ws

Follow her on Instagram: @lara.spadetto

Read also, by the same Author:
LET GO OF WHAT HURTS YOU
You can find it on Amazon and Kindle.

Special Thanks

I thank my children, Stefano, Filippo, and Ilaria, who pushed me to look beyond the limits I had set myself, and all the friends and family who supported me during the launch of my first book "Let Go Of What Hurts You".

Special thanks go to Jana S. Brown and Dane Cobain for the help they have given me, over the past few months, preparing this book.

Printed in Great Britain
by Amazon